Band Saw Pattern Book

Mark & Gene Duginske

Illustrations by Chris Morris & Marcia Blanco

 Sterling Publishing Co., Inc.   New York

Dedication

TO KATE MORRIS

Acknowledgments

We would like to thank the following people for their help with this book: Kate Morris (Mark's wife), Chris Morris for the computer drawings, Marcia Blanco for some of the freehand drawings, David Barwick, Garry Damp, Ed Hinsa, Barbara Reifschneider, Andrew Gilderson, David Morris, and Charles Nurnberg. We would also like to thank our editor.

Edited by R. P. Neumann

Library of Congress Cataloging-in-Publication Data

Duginske, Mark.
　　Band saw pattern book / Mark and Gene Duginske : illustrations by
Chris Morris.
　　　　p.　　cm.
　　Includes index.
　　ISBN 0-8069-8250-0
　　1. Woodwork.　　2. Band saws.　　I. Duginske, Gene.　　II. Title.
TTl85.D78　1991　　　　　　　　　　　　　　　　　　　　91-453
684'.083—dc20　　　　　　　　　　　　　　　　　　　　　　CIP

10　9　8　7　6　5　4　3

CONTENTS

INTRODUCTION

When making a woodworking project you will save time and wood if you have a clear idea of what you want to make. It is better to do the experimentation on paper rather than with wood. When the whole project is drawn on paper it is called a *plan*. Plans are either made by the woodworker or obtained from magazines and books. Full-sized plans can also be purchased. The individual shape of each piece in the plan is called a *pattern*. For example, the two-dimensional representation of a table leg on a piece of paper is referred to as the leg pattern.

This book provides two types of information. First, there are well over thirty plans for everyday household items. Second, the book provides sets of optional patterns for each piece of most of the items. This means that you already have a number of choices without having to go through the time and effort of creating your own options. By comparing the optional pattern designs you can also develop a good sense of the design process. It may even stimulate you to design your own patterns. By making many of the projects in this book and by studying the design options you can develop the skills needed to create your own plans and patterns from scratch.

This book is designed to help you learn how to use the band saw (and the scroll saw) by making a number of projects. Our intention is to provide plans that are useful rather than pure decoration. Our purpose is also to present the plans and patterns so that they provide an educational process. If you are not very experienced with the band saw, we suggest that you start with the projects towards the front of the book because these designs are the simplest.

You can progress towards the back of the book as you develop skill. It is not necessary that you make every project from front to back, but it would be good to have some solid experience before making the Queen Anne footstool or the Chippendale mirror.

If you are a more experienced woodworker, you can start with any project which suits your fancy. Although the focus is on plans and patterns, we also provide some hints as to the easiest means of construction. Since there are very few absolute rights and wrongs in woodworking, you can experiment with any project or type of construction that appeals to you.

A note of caution: do not be in a hurry and don't get frustrated if things don't turn out perfect the first time. The first time you make something, consider it as a learning experience and the piece as a prototype. As woodworkers we learn more from our mistakes than from any other process. To make something efficiently and of high quality takes the experience of a number of attempts. By the tenth time you make something, you will have the bugs worked out of your system.

This is our third band saw book and our first pattern book. The other two books are the *Band Saw Handbook* and *Band Saw Basics*. These books are about band saw adjustments, blades, and techniques. They are designed to help you gain skill and confidence with this wonderful machine. If you do not feel confident with either your skill or your machine, we suggest that you get one of these books.

Mark & Gene Duginske

1
USING PATTERNS

A woodworking project begins with an idea that is then drawn on a piece of paper to produce the plan. The plan includes the drawing of individual parts, each of which is called a pattern. The pattern is a two-dimensional representation that is either drawn directly on the workpiece or on a piece of paper that is attached to the workpiece with tape, rubber cement, or some form of spray mount. The band saw is then used to remove the waste on the outside of pattern lines.

Patterns are either created by the woodworker or obtained from magazines or books such as this one. There are also companies that sell full-sized patterns. Because of limited space the patterns in books or magazines are usually printed at a reduced size and covered with a reference grid that breaks the pattern down into easily transferred components. Usually the scale of the drawing is given in inches, giving a couple of dimensions to serve as reference. Enlarging the grid by hand is called *transposing*. Transposing is not difficult, especially after you've done it once.

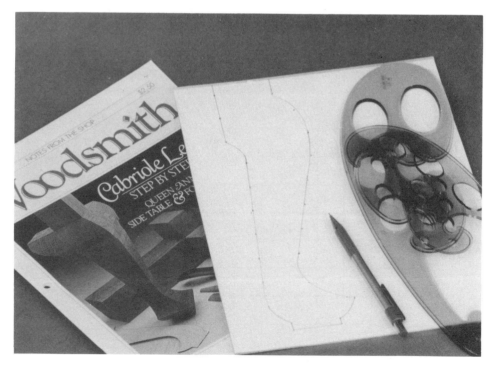

Books and magazines are a good source for patterns.

7

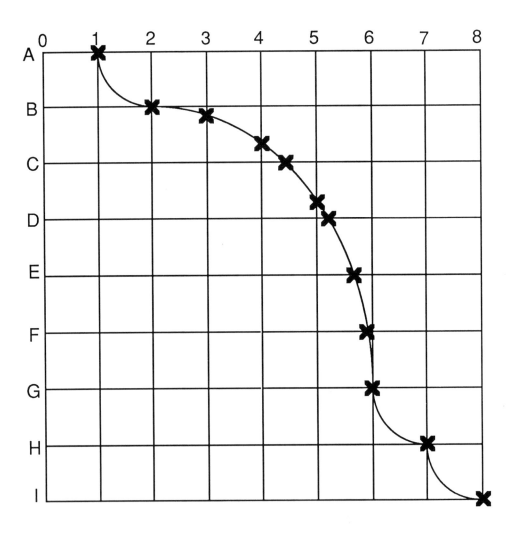

Transfer the pattern from the small grid to the large grid.

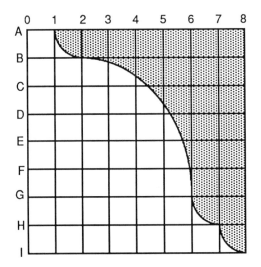

To make the full-sized plan the first step is to make a grid that is the desired size. You can use graph paper which already has grids or make your own grid on ordinary paper. Thick paper such as grocery bag paper works well. Make your grid so that it has the same number of squares as the pattern grid. By numbering and lettering the intersecting lines on each pattern it will be easy to transpose the intersecting lines from the small grid to the large grid. Mark the intersecting line with a dot or diagonal line. Use a french curve to connect the intersecting dots to create a smooth line. To avoid potential mistakes, we recommend that you start at one end and join the dots frequently, joining the straight lines first.

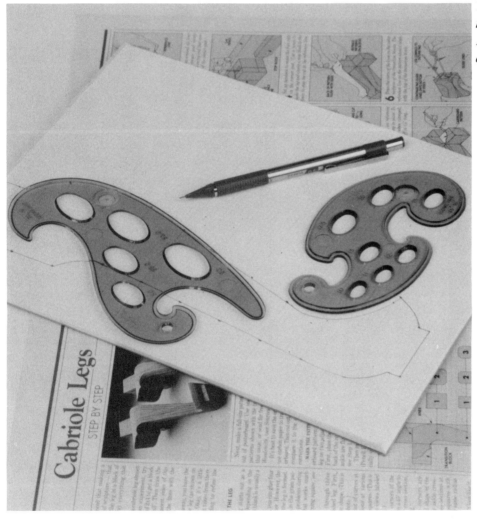

The dots are connected to complete the pattern. French curves help to create a smooth line.

The majority of the patterns in this book are overlaid by a square grid based on multiples of eight, having eight blocks on each side for a total of 64 squares. Some patterns use a grid that is half of that size or a quarter of that size. The advantage of using an eight-by-eight grid is that it is easy to change the size of the pattern and it is also very easy to make your own grid.

To make an eight-by-eight grid take a square piece of paper that is the desired pattern size, and fold it in half and then fold it in half again. Then fold the piece in half two more times. When you unfold the paper you will have a piece of paper with 16 squares. Using a ruler mark the middle of each square from both directions creating an X. Then make a pencil line on the folded lines and through the Xs to create a grid with 64 boxes.

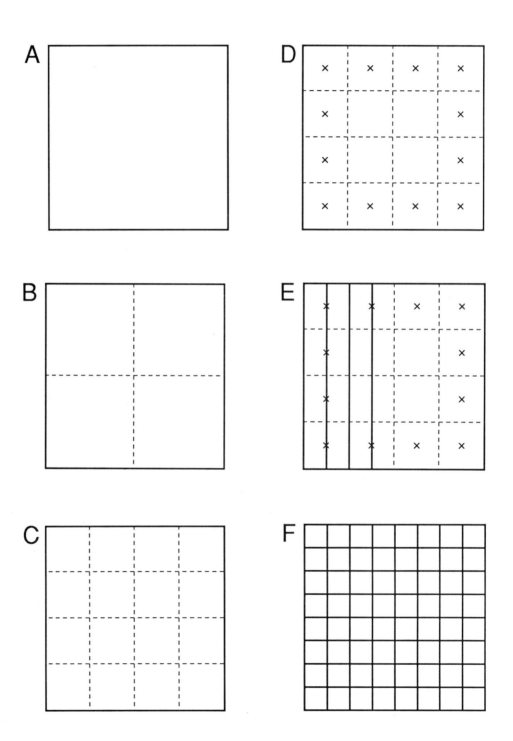

At times you may want to lengthen or shorten a pattern, such as a table leg design. By splicing the middle portion of the pattern you can make the leg either longer or shorter by adding or subtracting squares. This technique maintains the original proportions at each end. At other times you may want to elongate or shorten the whole pattern, not just the middle. This can be done by a process of changing the shape of the grid elements from square to rectangular.

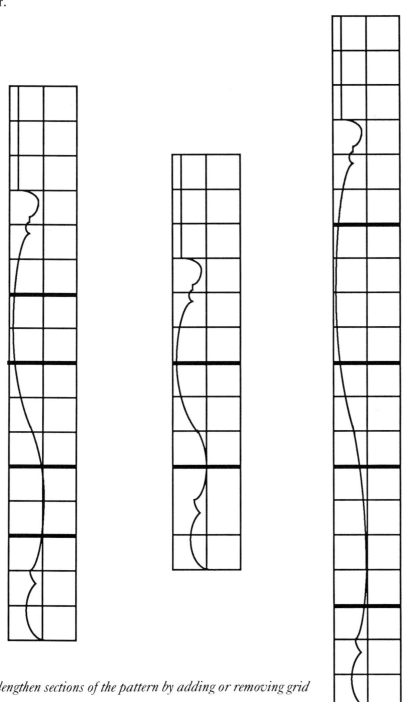

Shorten or lengthen sections of the pattern by adding or removing grid elements.

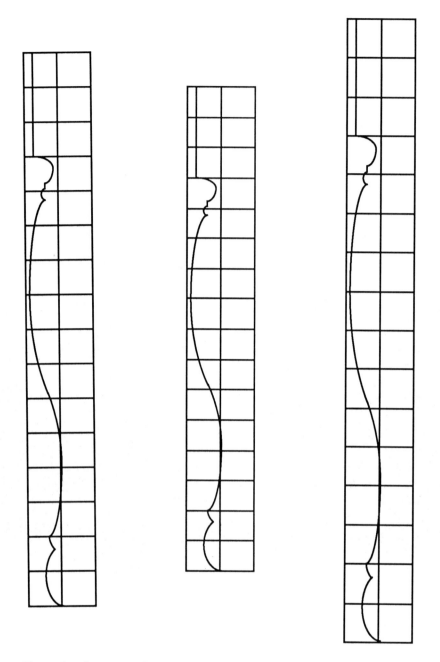

To maintain proportion when shrinking or expanding a pattern change the shape of the grid elements from square to rectangular.

There are other options for changing the pattern size. The easiest method is to use a photocopy machine which has the size-changing capability. Some machines can change the size of the pattern in one percent increments. Print shops use a technique called positive mechanical transfer (PMT) that can enlarge or shrink patterns while maintaining perfect proportion and clarity.

A mechanical drawing approach is accomplished with the use of the pantograph. The arms of the pantograph are adjustable, allowing a variety of ratios to be used.

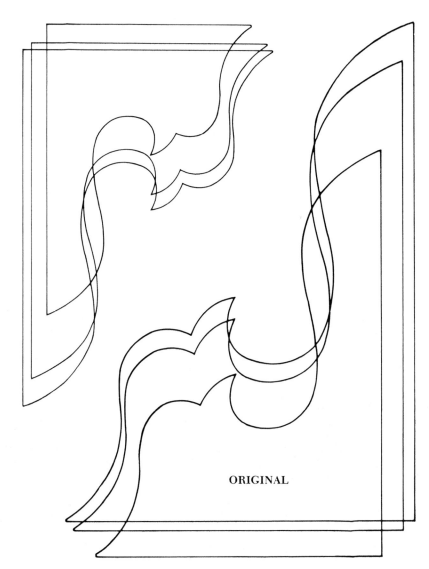

ORIGINAL

A photocopier was used to change the size of this design. The three sizes on the left are 93, 74, and 65 percent of the original. The two large designs on the right are 115 and 124 percent of the original, which is on the bottom right.

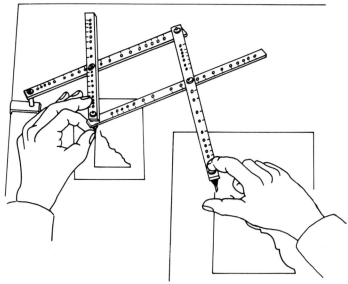

A pantograph is a mechanical device used to either enlarge or reduce a drawing. (Drawing courtesy of Lee Valley Tools, L.T.D., Ottawa, Canada)

Types of Pattern

Full Pattern

The full pattern as its name implies is a complete representation of the full pattern. The full pattern is used when the shape of the object is not symmetrical (that is, its proportions are not balanced). The pattern of a shelf bracket is an example of a full pattern.

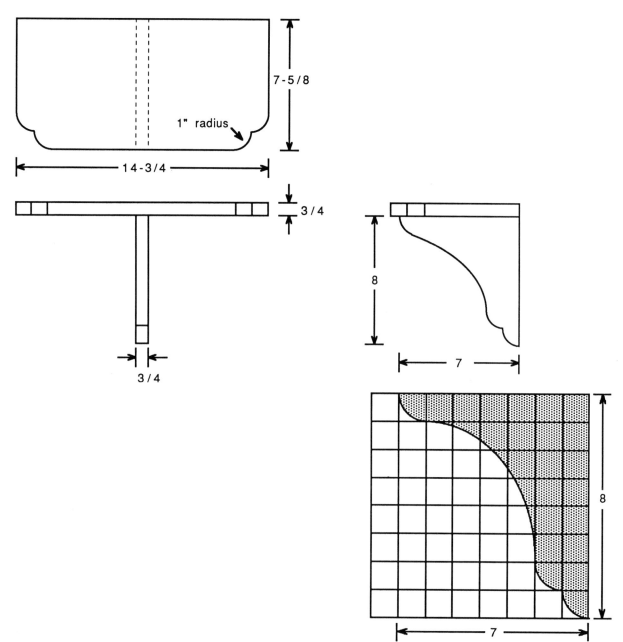

This is the full pattern of a shelf bracket, with a plan for the entire shelf given above.

Half-Pattern

When the object is symmetrical, it is possible to use a pattern that is only half of the shape. The half-pattern is best used on one side and then flipped over for the opposite side. This guarantees that both sides of the object will correspond exactly. The top of the shelf is a good example of a half-pattern.

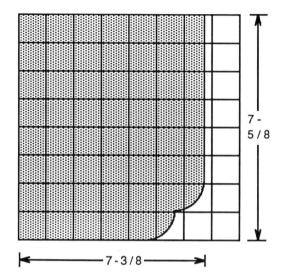

7 - 5 / 8

7 - 3 / 8

This is the half-pattern for the shelf.

Quarter-Pattern

An object that has four corners, each the same, can be made with a pattern that is the size of just one of the corners. The pattern is flipped left to right and then from top to bottom. A decorative tabletop is a good example of when a quarter-pattern can be used.

Double Pattern

An object that has the same profile from two adjacent sides, such as a cabriole leg, can be made by using the same pattern for each side.

Compound-Sawing

When there are patterns on two adjacent sides, two series of cuts are needed to release the workpiece. An example of compound-sawing is the boat hull shown below. After the pattern has been sawn from one side, the waste which has the pattern for the adjacent side is reattached. After the waste is reattached the piece is rotated and the second series of cuts is made. Hot-melt glue or tape works well for reattaching the waste with the pattern.

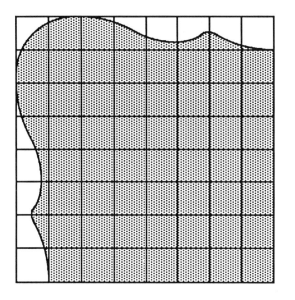

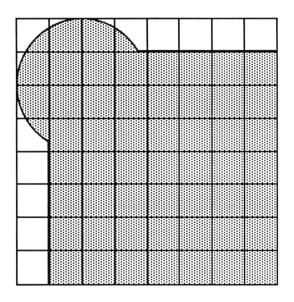

These are quarter-patterns, each for a different tabletop.

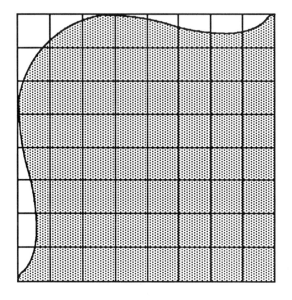

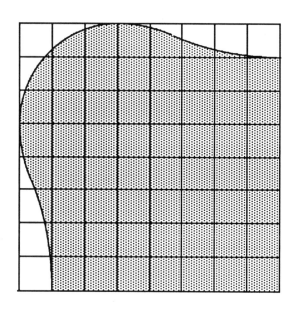

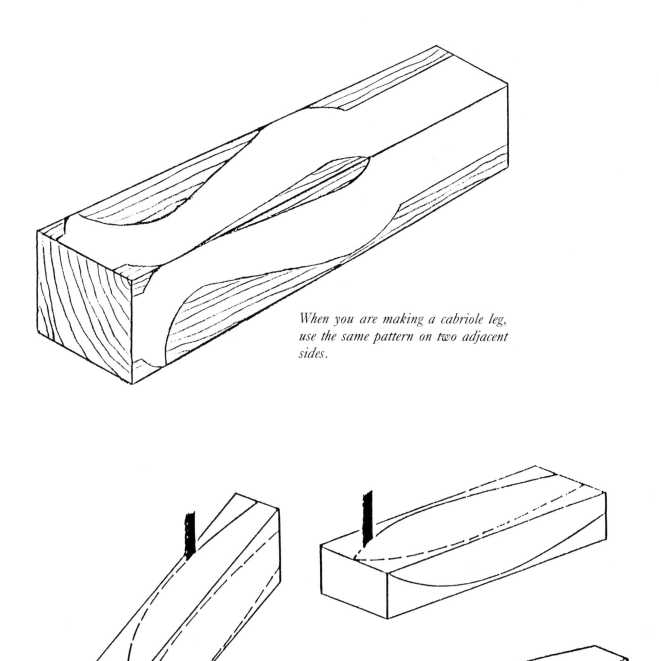

When you are making a cabriole leg, use the same pattern on two adjacent sides.

Here the pattern for a boat-model is being compound-sawed. In compound-sawing a pattern is cut from two adjacent sides. The second cut or series of cuts is made with the piece resting on its widest surface.

Creating Your Own Patterns

It is worthwhile to develop the skill of creating your own patterns. There are a number of techniques that you can use. If you are reproducing a part, as is often the case in furniture repair, you can sometimes use the original to trace a pattern. For example, a broken chair leg might be glued back together to provide the pattern for a replacement. If the piece cannot be used directly, a profile gauge may be used to transfer the shape. The sliding pins are pressed against the shape to be copied so that the exact outline can then be traced.

A profile gauge can be used to transfer a curved pattern.

At times you may wish to change existing patterns or create your own. With a few drafting tools and a little practice it is not difficult to develop this skill. Circles and parts of circles can be drawn with either a compass or a circle template. An ellipse template is used to make elliptical shapes or gentle curves. French curves are useful for making shapes that are neither circles nor ellipses. Adjustable rulers and curves make slight changes easy to accomplish. If you find that you really are serious about developing your own patterns, we suggest that you visit an art supply store or an office supply house to see what they have. Drafting tools, like all other tools, require a learning process.

Laying Out Patterns

When you locate the pattern on the work it is referred to as *layout*. Layout should be done carefully to avoid waste. It is best to lay out the pattern next to the edge of the board if possible. When laying out the pattern on the workpiece it is important to consider the direction of the grain so that maximum strength is achieved. If you are careful, you can place the patterns close together so that you will save material and time.

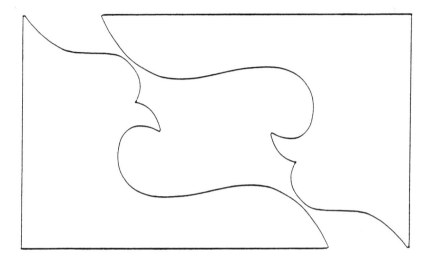

Putting patterns close together saves material by decreasing the waste.

Templates

Paper patterns are not very durable. If you are going to use a pattern often, it is worthwhile to make a template out of a more durable material such as Masonite™ (a type of fibreboard), plywood, or plastic. With a solid template it is easy to trace the pattern directly onto the workpiece. The best material is clear plastic that is about ⅛-inch thick. Because it is clear, you can see the grain of the wood under the pattern.

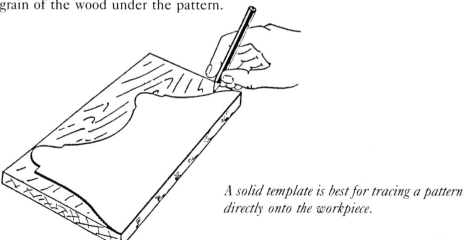

A solid template is best for tracing a pattern directly onto the workpiece.

The solid template helps you lay out the pattern on the workpiece for the best grain direction while minimizing the waste. Templates are useful for some large pieces where the pattern can be drawn on opposite sides of the workpiece.

Pattern-Sawing

Pattern-sawing is a technique that can be used to make multiple pieces that are identical. A solid pattern is attached to the workpiece. The waste is removed by guiding the pattern near the saw blade with a "rub block." A plywood pattern is best, because it will not shrink or expand. The blade is housed in the rub block so that the cut is made about 1/16 inch to 1/8 inch from the pattern.

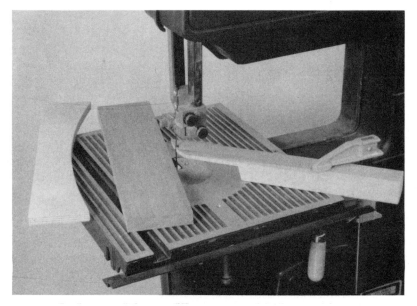

Make the rub block so that the workpiece can slide under it. Clamp the rub block to the table with the opposite end surrounding the blade.

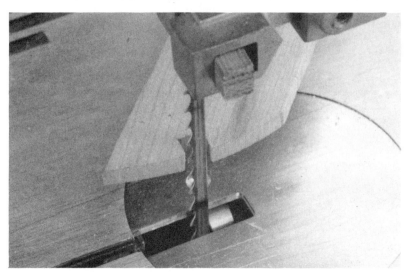

The rub block should have a curved end with a notch. The notch in the rub block fits over the blade and protrudes past it about 1/16 inch.

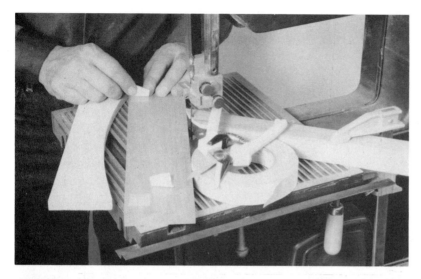

Use double-faced tape to attach the solid pattern to the workpiece. Hot-melt glue or brads could be used rather than the tape.

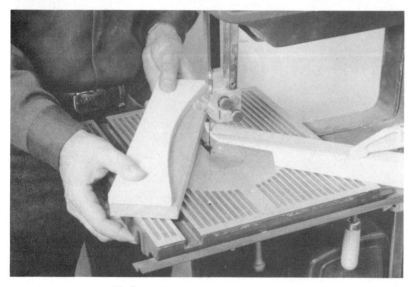

Press the solid pattern firmly onto the tape. A one-inch square piece of tape on each end of the pattern is usually enough. If you use too much tape or glue it may be very hard to remove the solid pattern.

Begin the cut with the solid pattern touching the rub block.

21

As you continue cutting, use slight pressure to keep the solid pattern against the rub block.

The completed cut. The workpiece should extend about $1/16$ inch past the pattern.

The waste is then trimmed off using a flush-cutting router bit which has a bearing on top of it. The bearing contacts the pattern and the waste is removed by the router bit.

Since the router bit will cut exactly the shape of the pattern, it is important that the pattern be as smooth as is possible. The pattern can be attached with hot-melt glue, brads, or double-faced tape. Besides being useful when you have to make a number of pieces that are exactly the same, this technique can be used for curves that are as small as the size of the flush-cutting router bit. If the pattern has details that are smaller than the diameter of the router bit, an alternative method must be used.

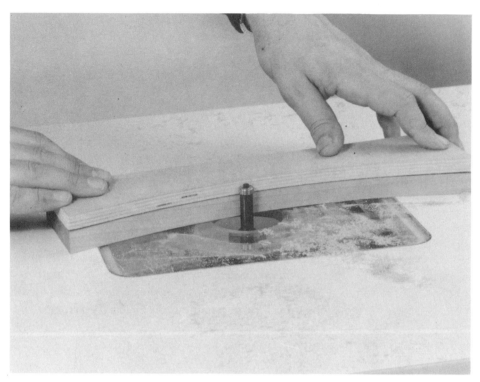

While the solid pattern piece is still attached to the workpiece trim off the waste with a router. The router bit being used for this operation is called a flush-cutting bit. The bearing on top of the bit is the same size as the cutter and rides against the solid pattern.

2
BASIC PROJECTS

This first section of patterns is designed to provide you with basic projects that are easy to make. These projects are typically cutouts made of single pieces of wood. In some cases a project may requires pieces laminated together. There is no requirement to fit the pieces together in any precise way. There is a lot of leeway in assembling the laminated pieces. If you are just starting to use the band saw, we suggest that you start with some of these basic projects before you attempt projects in the later chapters.

Interior Cuts

Some numbers and letters such as the letter P have a negative or empty space which must be removed. Wood-cutting band saws are not designed to do interior cuts. Some metal-cutting band saws have welders so that the blade can be cut and rewelded inside a hole. Of course you could also use a scroll saw or a sabre saw to make the interior cut. In some cases it is possible to drill a hole rather than make a cut. However, with some planning you can make and sand interior cuts with the band saw.

To start the interior cut with the band saw, make the entry cut. If it is a straight cut use the rip fence or mitre guide to position the work if possible.

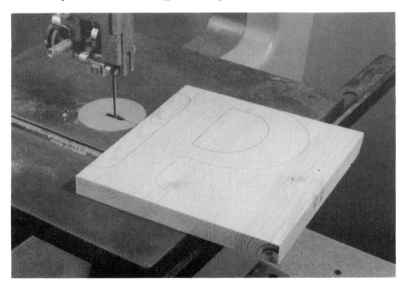

The letter P is marked on the wood in pencil.

24

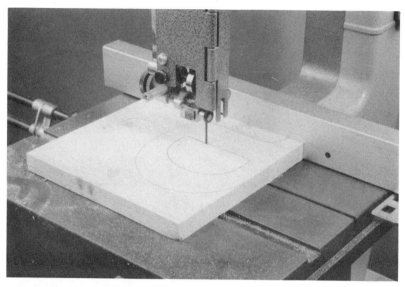

Make the straight entry cut by using the rip fence or mitre guide if possible.

Remove the waste.

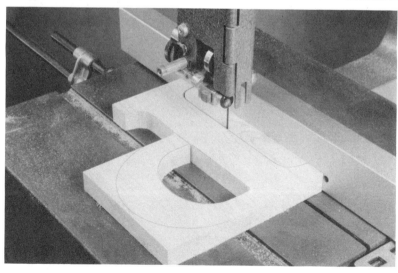

Use the rip fence or the mitre guide to make the opposite straight cut, and remove the rest of the waste.

There are two options for dealing with the kerf left from the entry cut. You can just leave it open which is simplest, or you can glue the seam back together. If the piece of wood is large and flexible (as pine, for instance) you can just put glue in the crevice and clamp it together. Otherwise, glue a thin strip of wood in place to make up for the kerf.

Leave a square corner on the outside of the piece so that there is sufficient support for clamping the work. After the glue dries release the clamp and finish the outside of the piece.

Leave a corner uncut so that there is a support for the clamp.

Wait for the excess glue to dry. Then remove it with a sharp chisel.

Remove the clamp and finish cutting the waste from the piece.

Letters and Numbers

These patterns for letters and numbers are slightly angled, which is more decorative than square designs. To change the size of these letter and number patterns, you can use the grid method but the easiest way to do it is on a copying machine. These designs are usually made with a 1/8-inch or 1/16-inch blade. If you have a mitre guide, you may want to use it to maintain consistency for some of the angles.

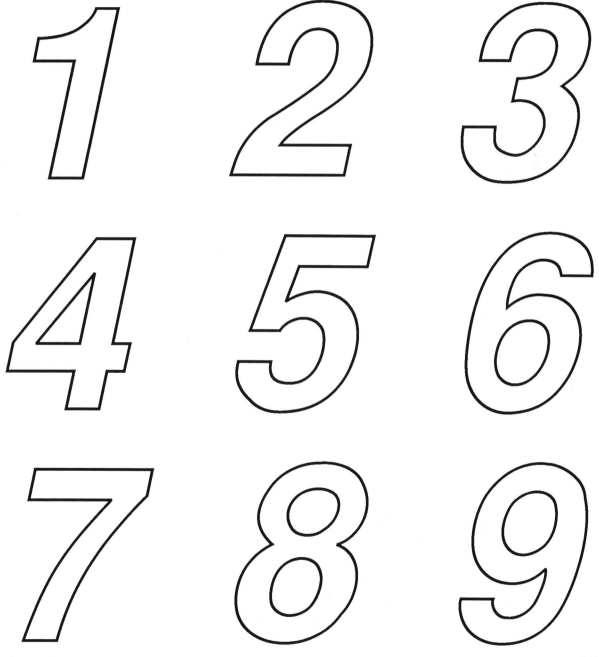

a b c

g h i j

n o p

28

d e f

k l m

q r s t

29

930140

u v w

x y

z

A B C

D E

F G H

Animals

Animal patterns can be used to make pieces for a number of different purposes. The finished pieces can be used as decoration, especially folk art decoration. These patterns can also be used for making cutting boards, boxes, containers, and toys.

This swan has been made of aromatic cedar and is designed to hang over the closet rod. Cedar is a well-known alternative to moth balls.

This fox puzzle was made with a ¹⁄₁₆-inch blade.

Kerfing

Kerfing is a technique used to curve wood. Kerfing is done by making a series of incomplete cuts. About 1/16 inch of the wood remains. The wood has the flexible characteristics of veneer which allows the piece to bend in either direction. If you glue a piece of veneer to the kerfed side, the dried piece will hold the desired curve and will be very strong.

Kerfing is done by making a series of incomplete cuts.

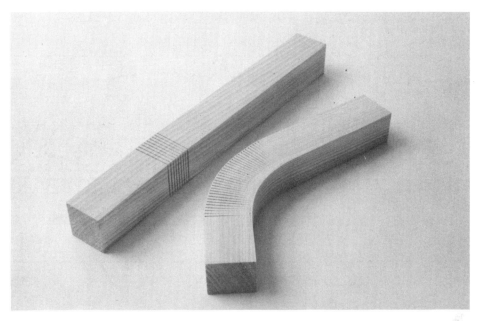

When a piece of veneer is glued to the kerfed side, the piece maintains the curve of the bending form.

You can also glue canvas to the wood before making the kerf cuts. This makes the resulting piece even more flexible, without the potential for breakage. You can also glue the canvas between two boards and then make the kerf cuts. This makes the piece very flexible in both directions. This techique was used to make the toy dinosaur.

This toy dinosaur is made from two kerfed boards with a piece of canvas glued between them.

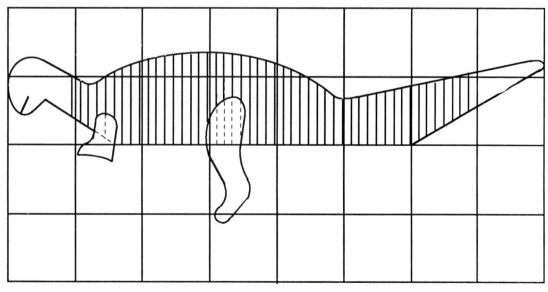

Toy dinosaur pattern. The side of each square is equal to one inch.

Folk Art Piggy Bank

We believe that every child should have a piggy bank. This design can be made from a scrap of two-by-six lumber. The outside pieces are cut on a slight bevel which requires tilting the table. The legs are square. Cloth or leather ears would add something to this pig's beauty.

Folk art piggy bank.

The piggy bank is made out of three pieces of wood. The best blade to use is a ⅛ inch blade with fourteen teeth per inch (TPI). The middle piece should be 1½-inches thick and can be made from a piece of scrap of two-by-four lumber. After the outside of the piece is cut, the inside is removed. The grain of the middle piece should run from front to back. Make the sides from material that is ¾-inch thick with the grain running from top to bottom.

The material between the front and back legs can be cut from both pieces at the same time with the table at 90 degrees to the blade. The remaining waste should be removed from each piece with the table tilted at seven degrees. The angled cut will give the pig a more realistic, rounded look. If possible, you might want to add the cloth or leather ears.

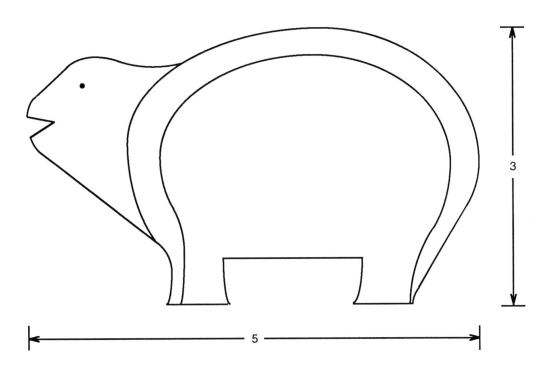

Bird Stamp Holder

The stamp holder in the shape of a bird is similar to the piggy bank except that there are two openings. The large opening is for inserting the stamp role, and the small opening at the mouth is the exit for the individual stamps. Cut the outside of the three pieces at the same time for the best results. After the outside is cut, the inside of the middle piece is cut or drilled out. Make the saw cut at the mouth last.

Because the breast of the bird is loose it should be taped to the larger piece before gluing the sides. Use toothpicks to keep the mouth open at the desired spacing. Run the tape all of the way around the middle piece so that the breast is held secure.

Bird stamp holder.

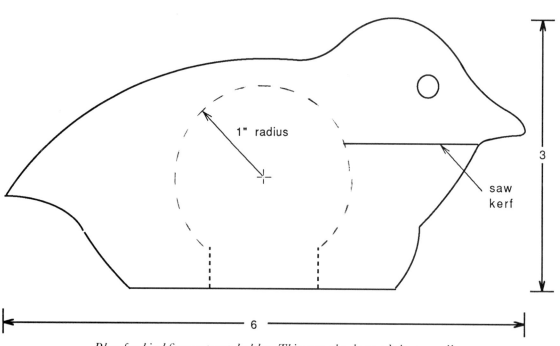

1" radius

saw
kerf

3

6

Plan for bird figure stamp holder. This can also be made in a smaller size.

49

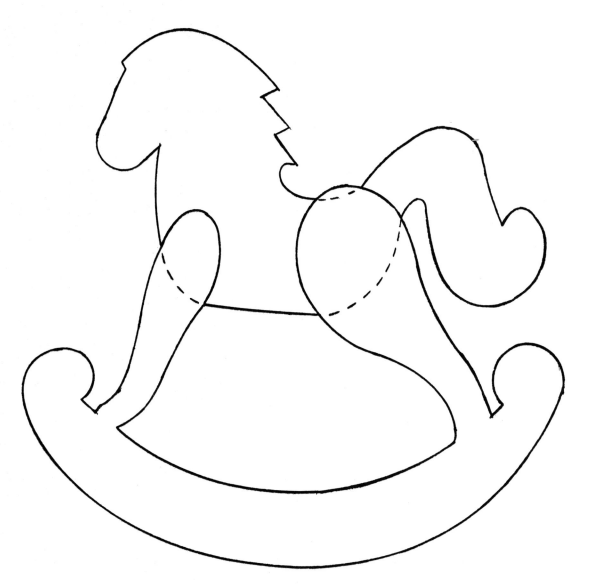

Laminated horse plan.

Decorative Patterns

These patterns are decorative designs that can be used for a multitude of purposes. The designs can be rotated for different uses and to generate design ideas. By using the pattern as a half-pattern the options are expanded.

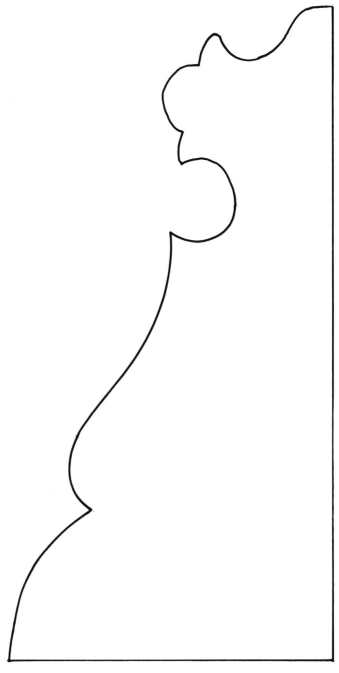

This design in the vertical position would be useful for a number of purposes such as the bracket for a shelf.

The design might then suggest a use for decoration such as the top of a mirror. A tabletop might come to mind, for example, from the use of the pattern as a quarter-pattern. Patterns such as these have many potential applications; the projects in subsequent chapters are one option for the use of these decorative patterns.

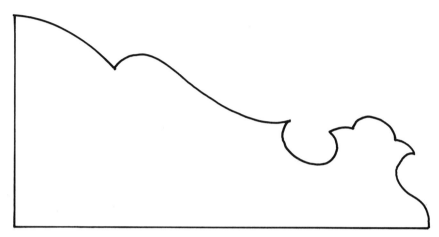

This reduced pattern is in the horizontal position.

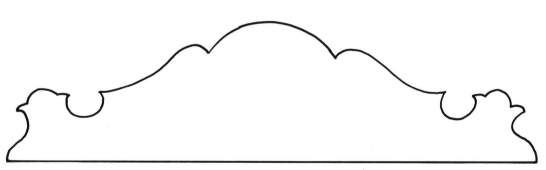

By using the pattern as a half-pattern, a wide design (reduced again) is created that would be useful as a decorative top for a mirror.

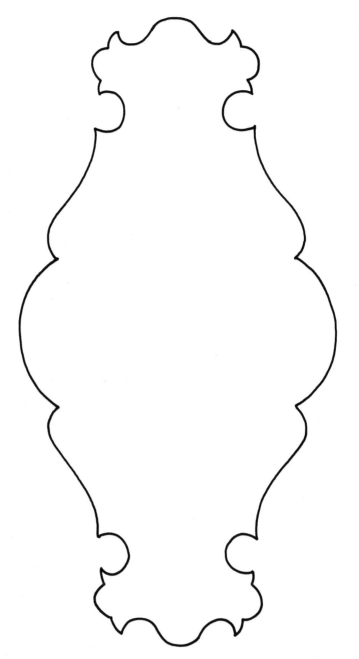

This design is made with the pattern used as a quarter-pattern.

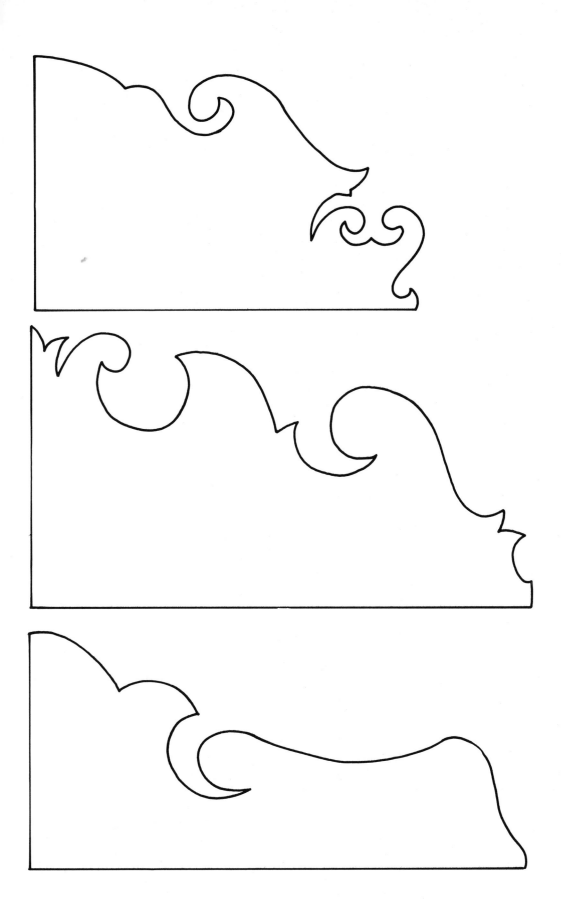

57

58

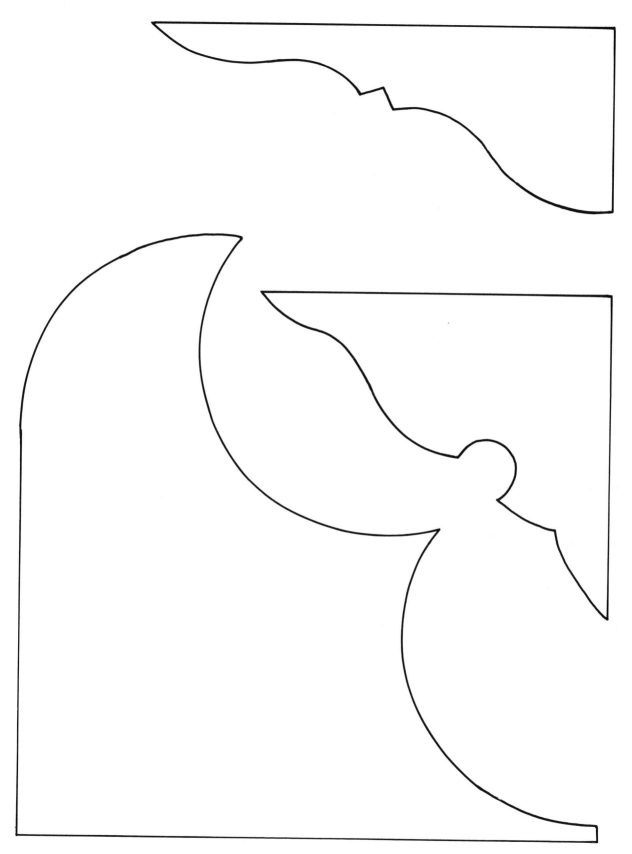

59

60

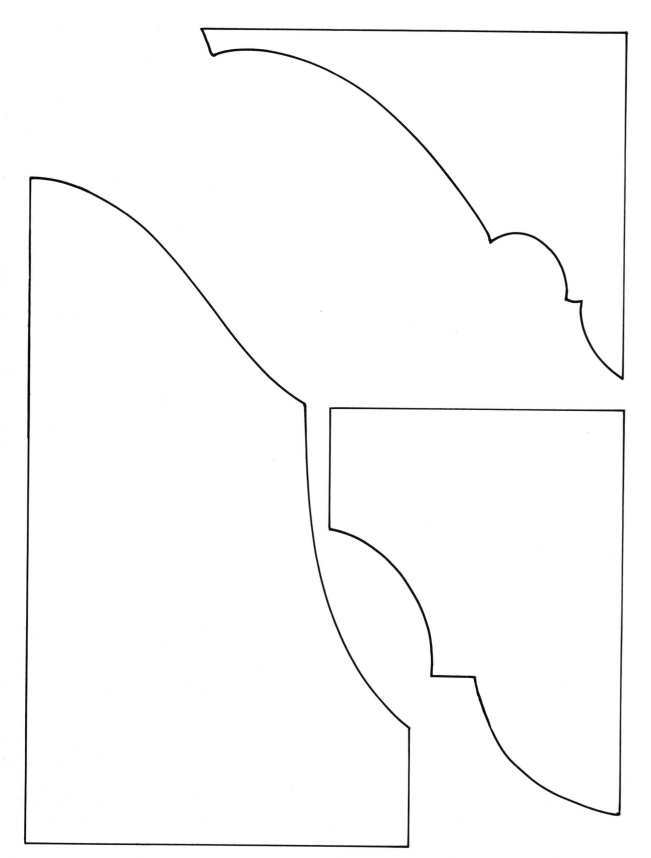

61

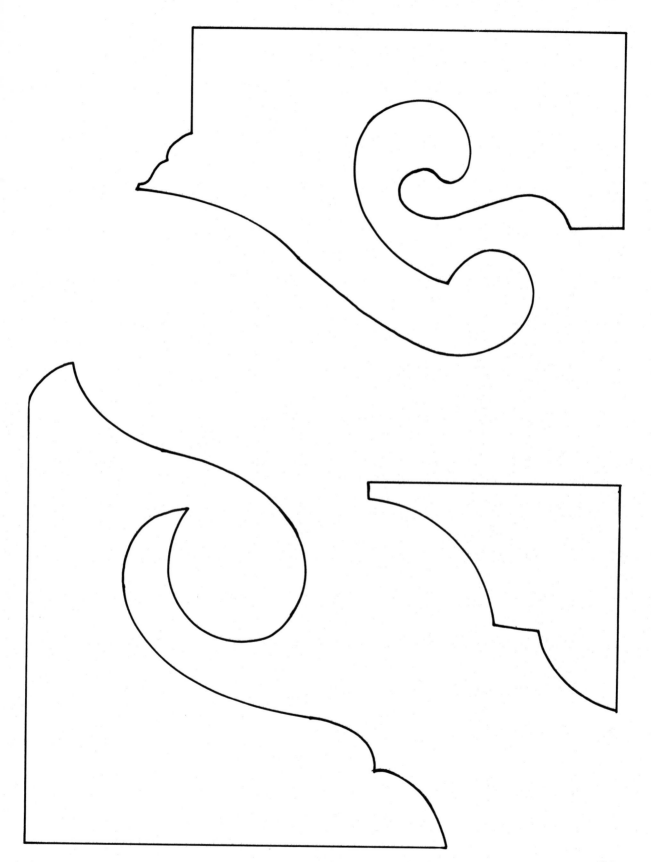

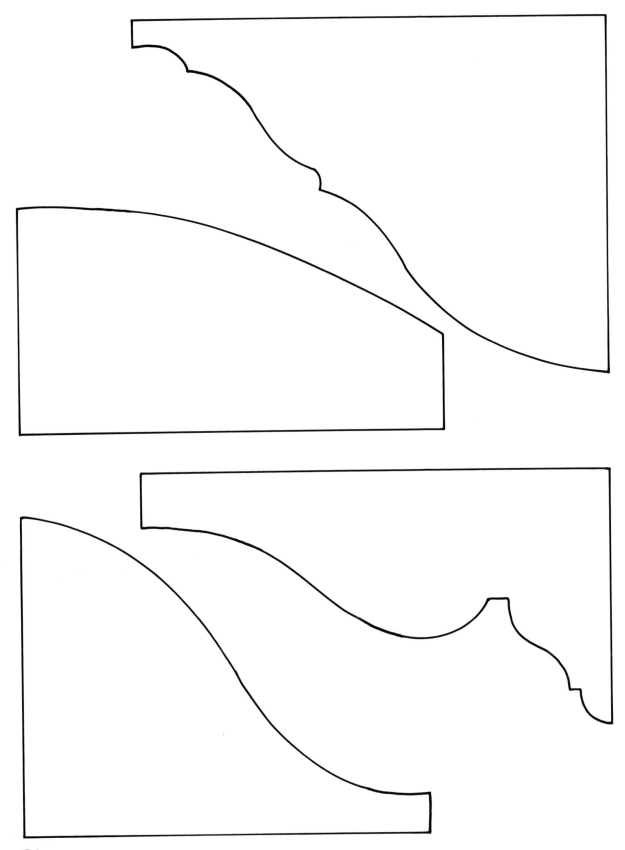

66

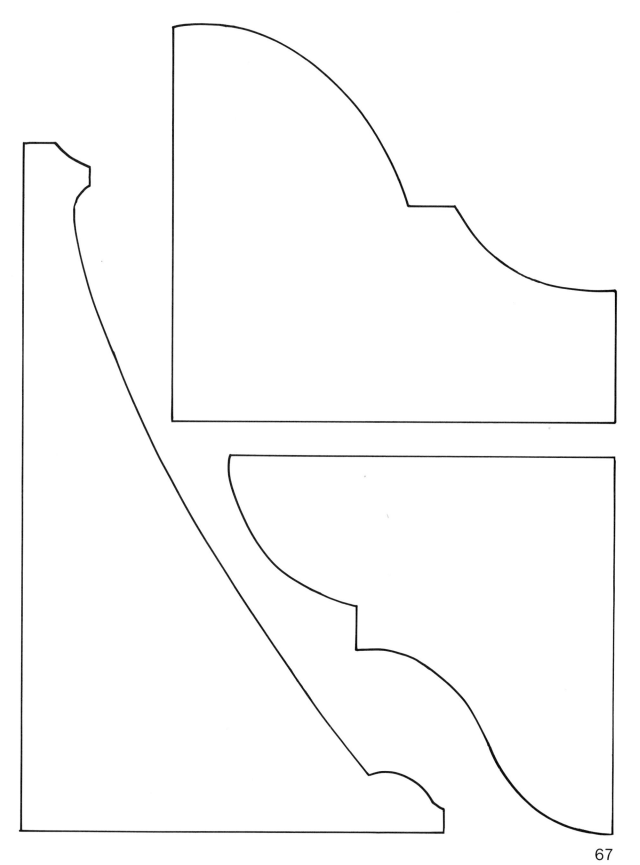

67

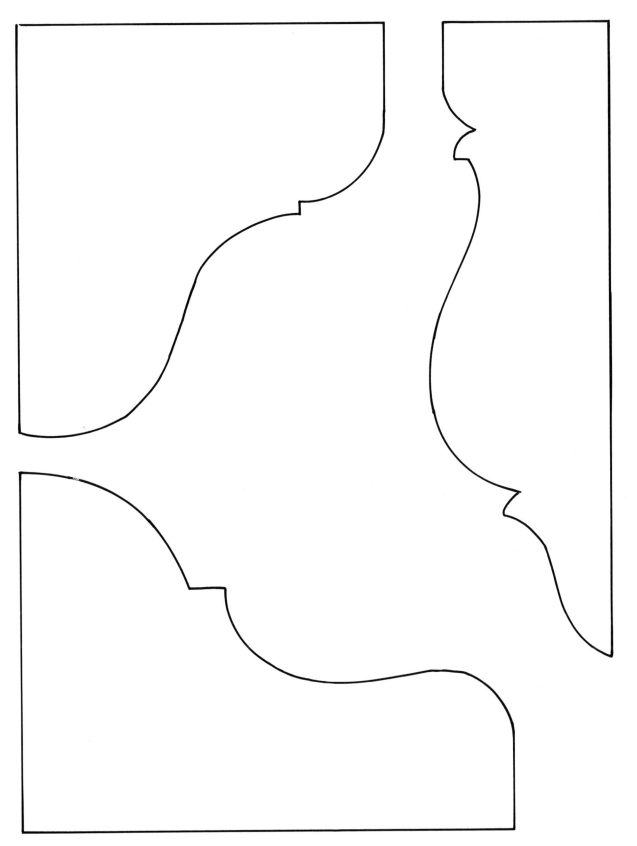

68

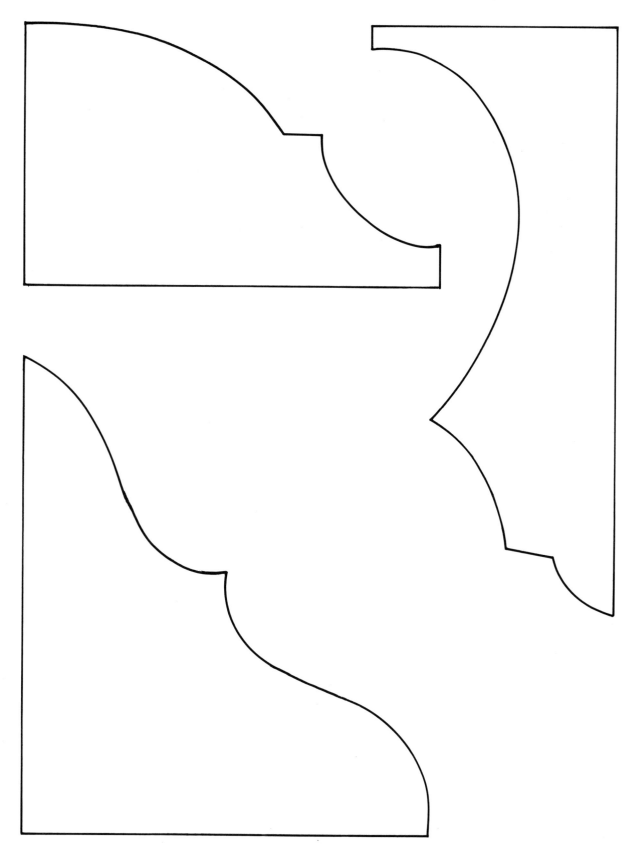

69

70

73

Hand Mirror

The hand mirror is a simple project that is easy to make. This one is made of walnut. The small round mirrors are glued to the wood after the finish has dried completely. These mirrors are available from glass supply houses or can be ordered from catalogues or from companies that advertise in woodworking magazines.

Walnut hand mirror.

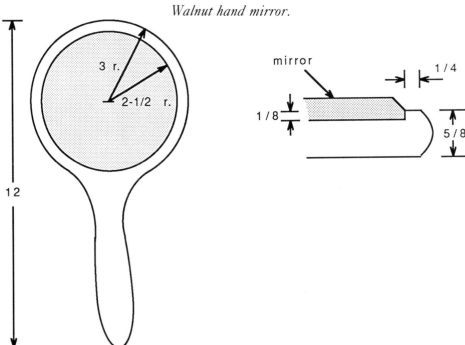

Pattern of the walnut hand mirror. You have the option of recessing the mirror if you choose.

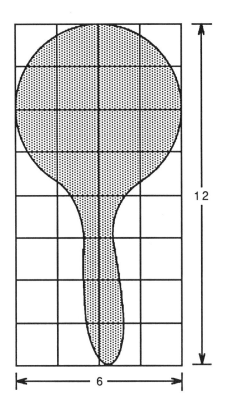

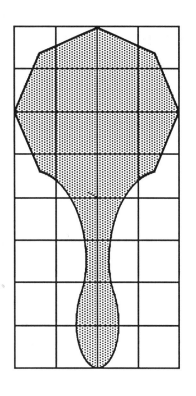

Hand mirror patterns.

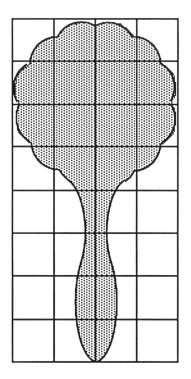

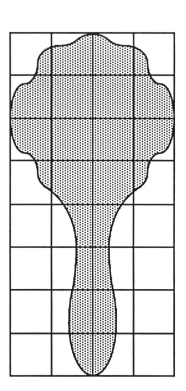

Small Wall Shelf

This small wall shelf is a good beginning project because it only requires that you cut two boards. The top is made with the use of a half-pattern. Many variations are provided for the half-pattern. Another option is to use two brackets to support the top rather than one. Many variations are also provided for the bracket pattern.

Shelf with single bracket, made from butternut.

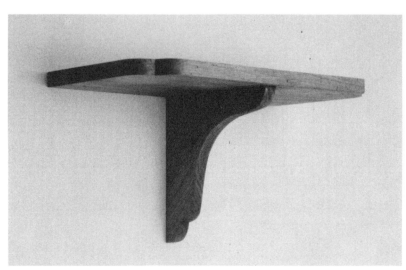

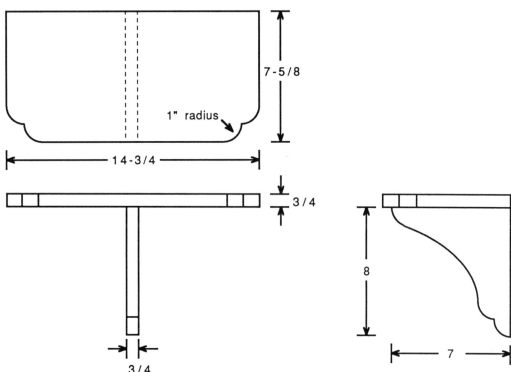

7-5/8

1" radius

14-3/4

3/4

3/4

8

7

Plan for a single bracket shelf. An option with this design is to use two brackets.

The bracket requires an 8-inch by 8-inch grid. The top requires a grid 7⅝-inch square for the half-pattern. The pieces can be joined by the use of a dado, a sliding dovetail, or simply a series of screws. The screw holes should be filled with plugs cut from the same material.

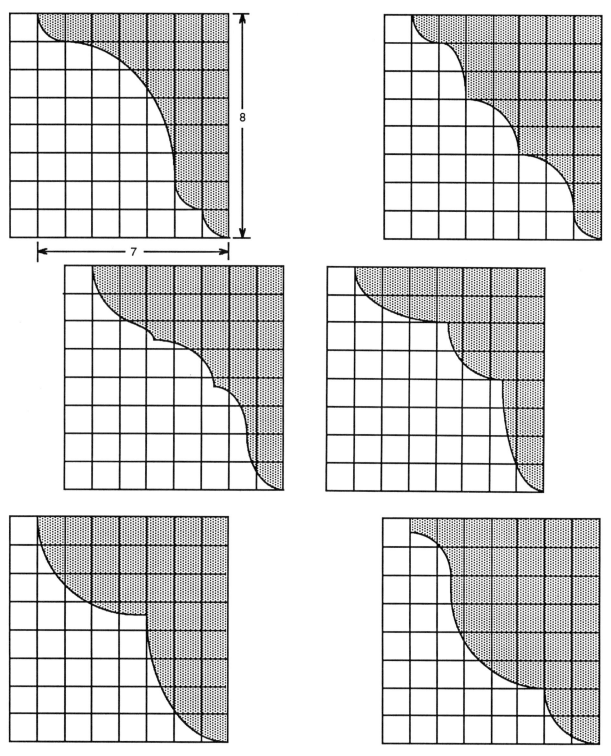

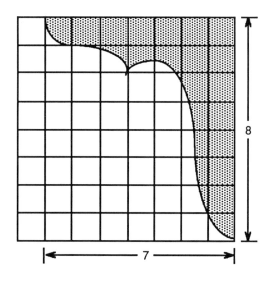

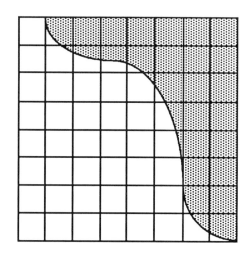

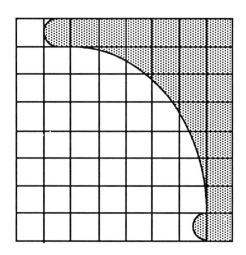

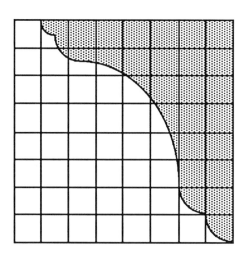

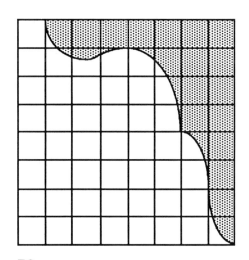

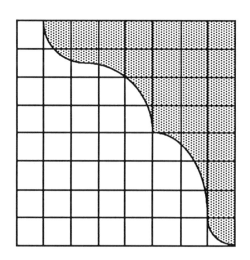

78

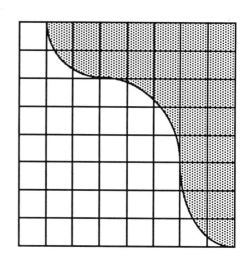

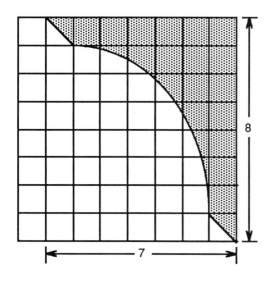

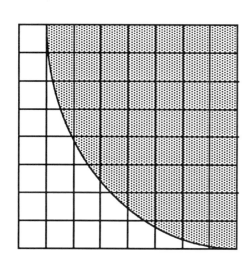

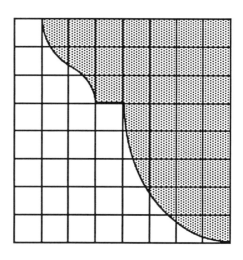

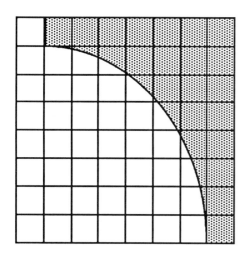

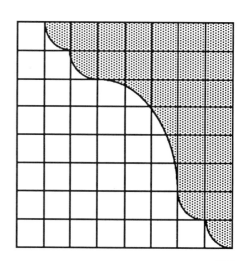

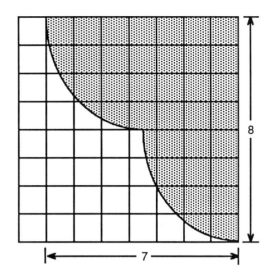

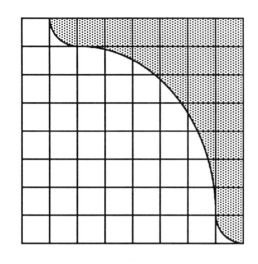

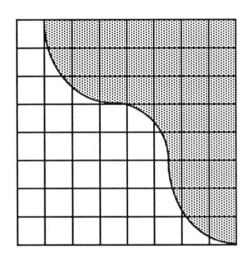

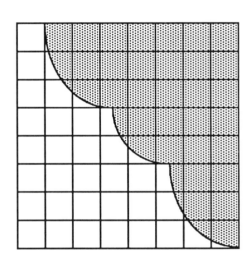

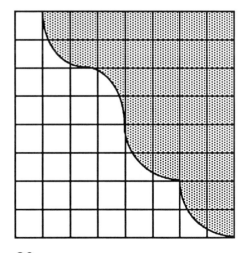

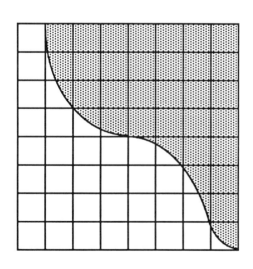

80

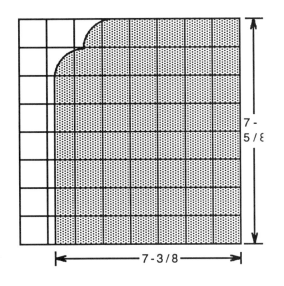

7 - 5/8

7-3/8

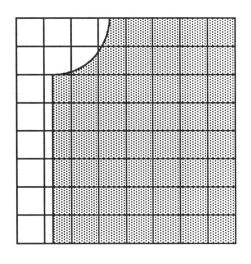

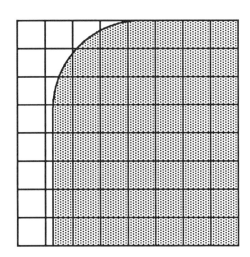

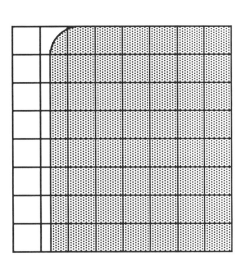

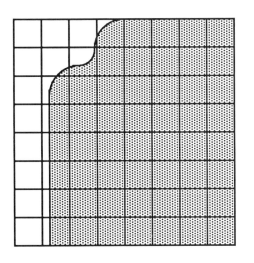

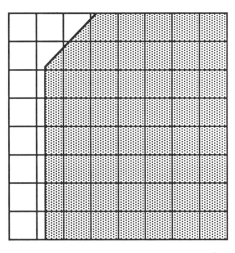

Cutting Boards

Cutting boards made of different colored woods are an attractive use of your band-saw skills. As well the project produces a useful result, and it is a good way to use up any scrap wood that you may have accumulated. The curved lines are made with a flexible ruler or with a curved yardstick.

Cutting board in walnut, maple, and cherry

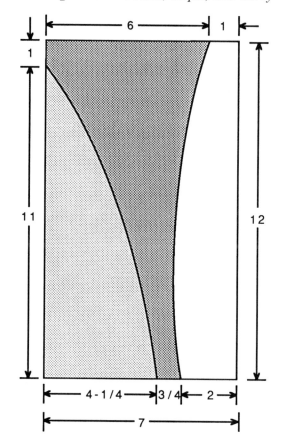

One very simple technique is to cut a stack of boards of different colors, and then glue the boards back together, edge to edge, alternating the colors. If you stack three different-colored boards, and then make two cuts, you will have three cut boards that have a similar design but vary in color.

Hold the starting pieces together with narrow strips of double-faced tape. Use a ½-inch hook-tooth blade with a pitch of 3 teeth per inch (TPI) to make the cuts. After the cuts are made, gently sand the cut surface to remove any roughness. However, be careful not to remove too much material or the pieces will not fit tightly. Also be careful not to round the edges.

These pieces are being held together with double-faced tape. The cuts were made with a ½-inch hook-tooth blade with a pitch of 3 teeth per inch (TPI).

Separate the pieces from each other and then glue them together.

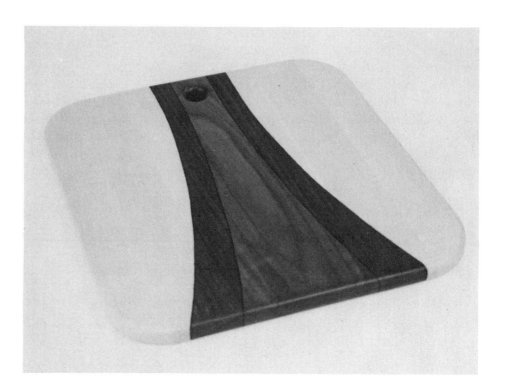

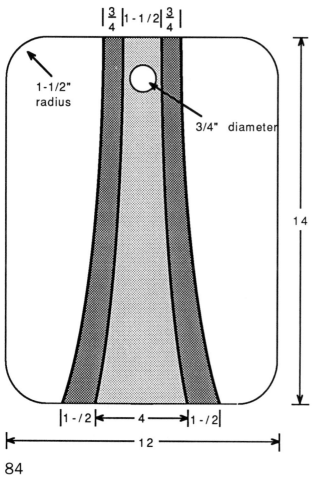

$\frac{3}{4}$ | 1-1/2 | $\frac{3}{4}$

1-1/2"
radius

3/4" diameter

14

1-/2 | 4 | 1-/2

12

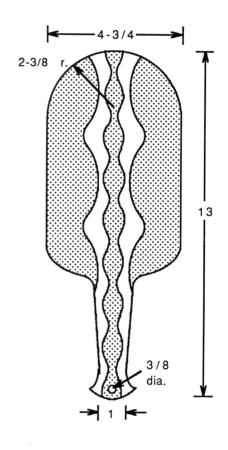

4-3/4

2-3/8 r.

13

3/8 dia.

1

84

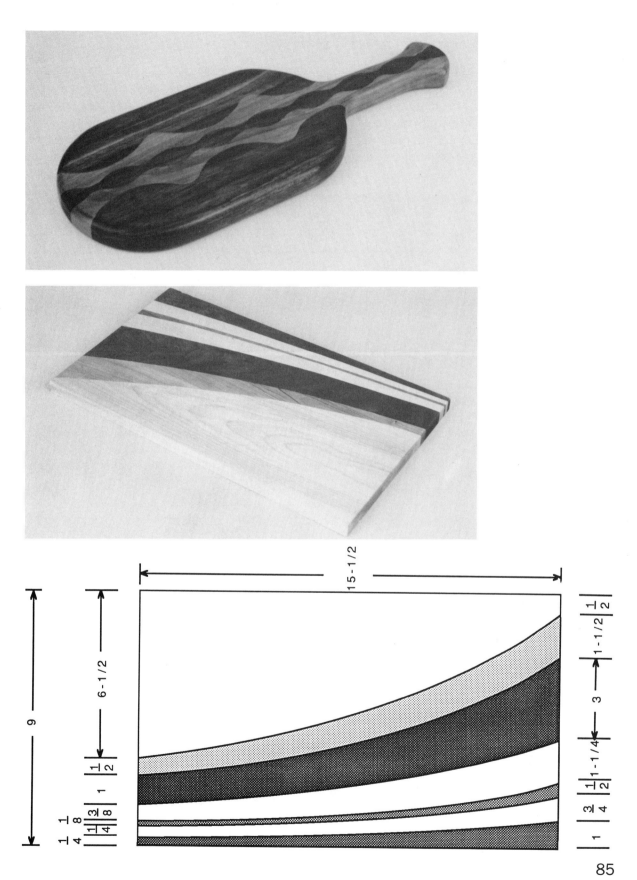

85

Plaques and Frames

Plaques and frames are made on the band saw using a quarter- or half-pattern. After the edge is sanded, the usual procedure is to put a decorative edge along the outside with a router.

Frames are made by using a cut-and-glue technique. The pieces to be cut for the two halves are attached face to face using double-faced tape or with

Wood plaques made with the use of a quarter-pattern. The decorative edge is made with a router.

Frame made with the band saw using the cut-and-glue technique.

hot-melt glue. The middle is then cut out. The halves are glued together using dowels for proper aligning. After the glue has dried, a rabbet is made in the back using a rabbeting router bit. The rabbet is made to accept the mirror or the picture.

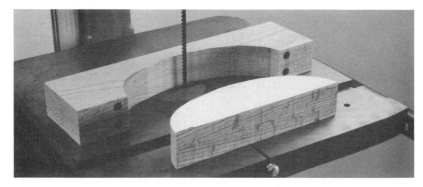

Using a half-pattern and the cut-and-glue technique.

The dowels help to align the two halves after the inside is sanded. After gluing, cut the final outside shape.

7-1/4

3/4" STOCK

11-3/4

7/16 GROOVE

A rabbetted groove is made in the back of the frame with a rabbeting router bit. The rabbet is made to accept the mirror or the picture and glass.

87

Plans for frame using an eight-by-sixteen grid.

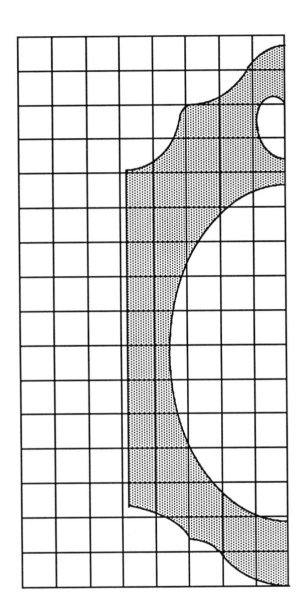
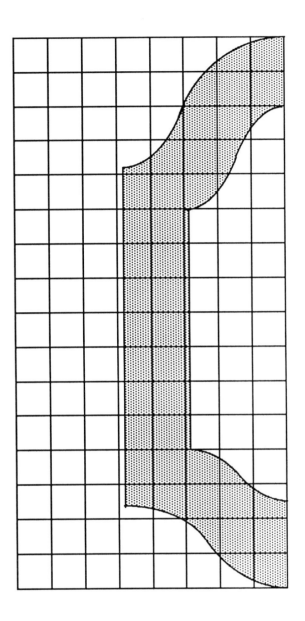

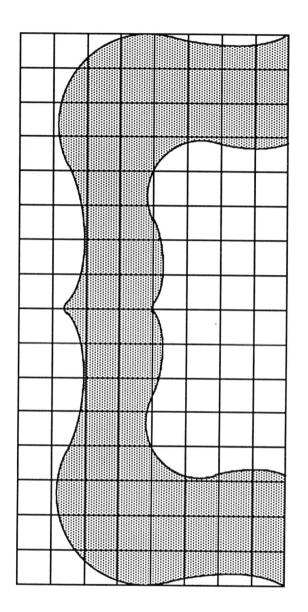

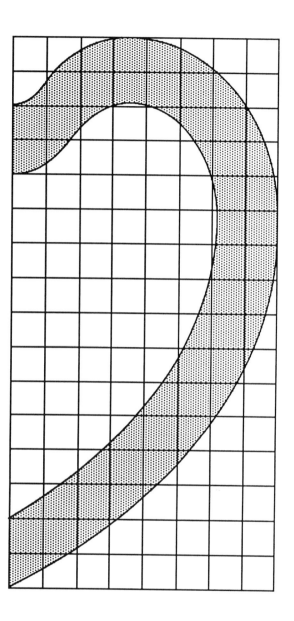

89

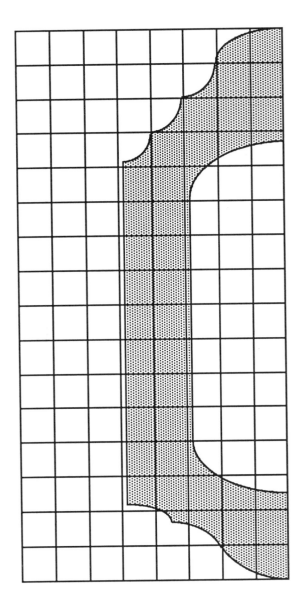
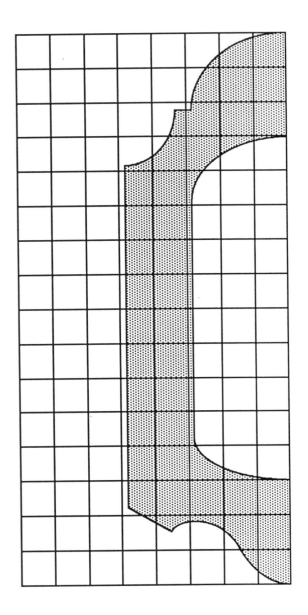

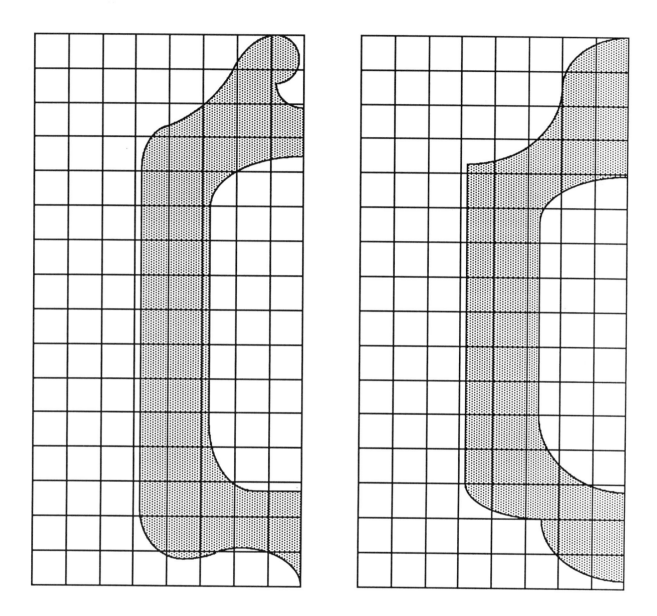

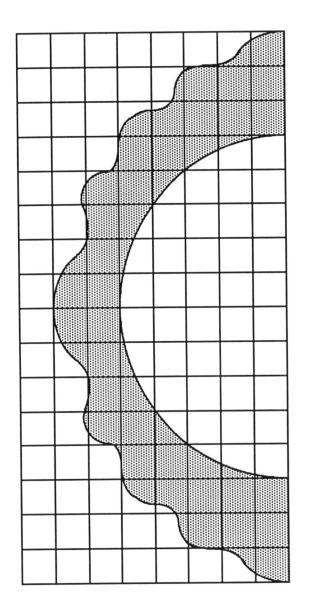
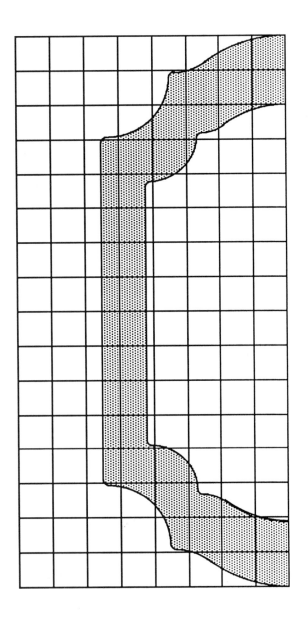

92

If you decide that you would like to make a mirror, you may find that you have problems cutting the glass for the shape of the frame. An option is to use plastic mirror material, which is available from glass or plastic supply houses. This material cuts like regular plastic. Mark the material using the frame. The best blade is the ⅛-inch fourteen teeth per inch (TPI) blade. Feed the plastic slowly into the blade so that the material does not melt behind the cut. This material will allow you to make a mirror of any shape that you choose.

Use the frame to mark the plastic mirror material.

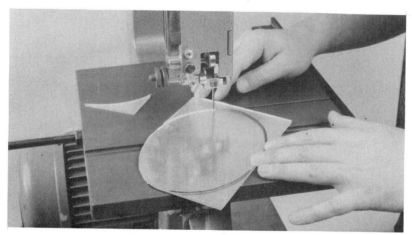

Use a ⅛-inch fourteen teeth per inch (TPI) blade to cut the plastic mirror material. It is best to use a slow feed so that the plastic does not melt back together after the cut.

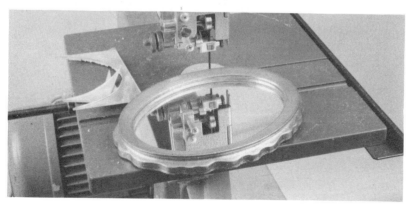

The plastic mirror material allows you to make a mirror of any shape.

Wood Toys

The band saw is the tool of choice for making toys. The toys can be simple, such as one-piece cars and trucks, or more complex such as planes and boats. The toys should be designed so that there are no sharp edges. The wheels can either be purchased or they can be made with the band saw using a circle-cutting jig.

These toys are made with light and dark woods which help to make them more appealing. Toys should be rounded to prevent injury to small children.

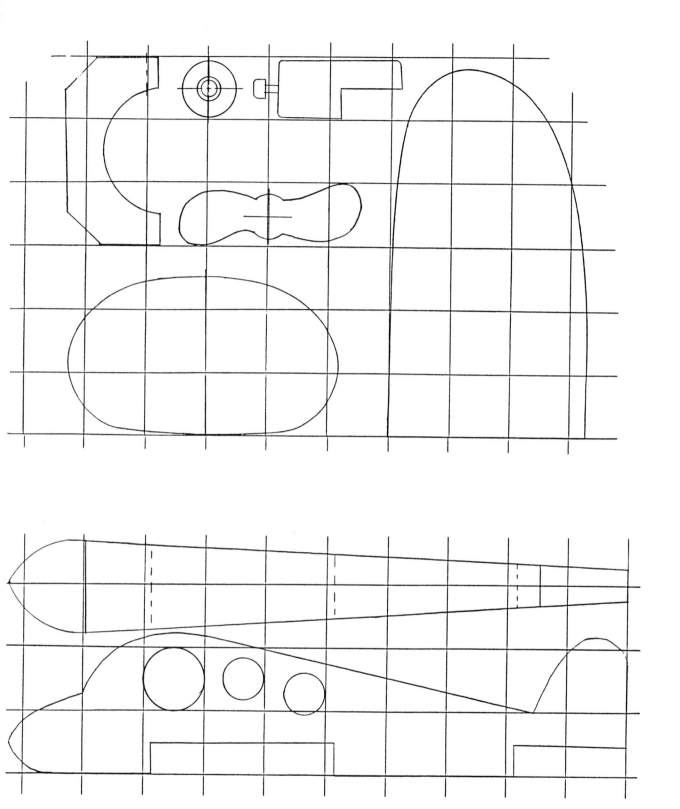

Plan for the plane; the side of each square represents one inch.

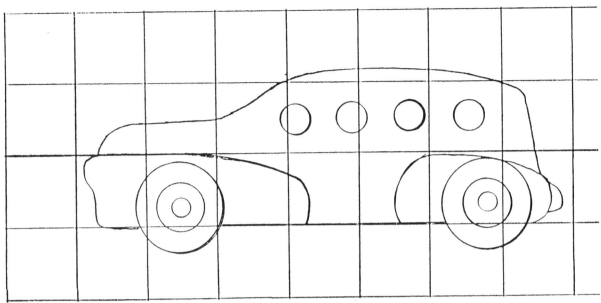

Car pattern, the side of each square equals ¾ inch.

These one piece toy cars are made of scrap pine and maple. The wheels are made on the band saw using a circle-cutting jig.

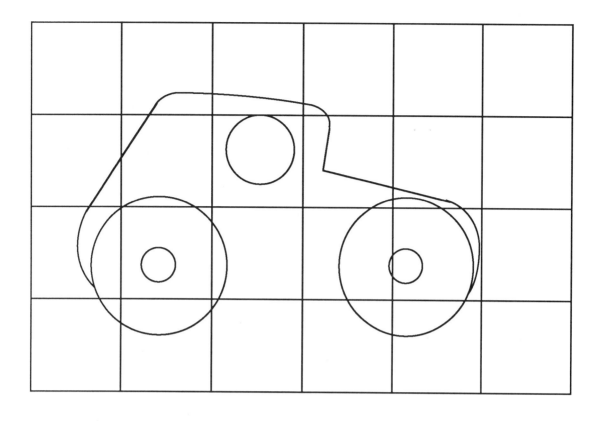

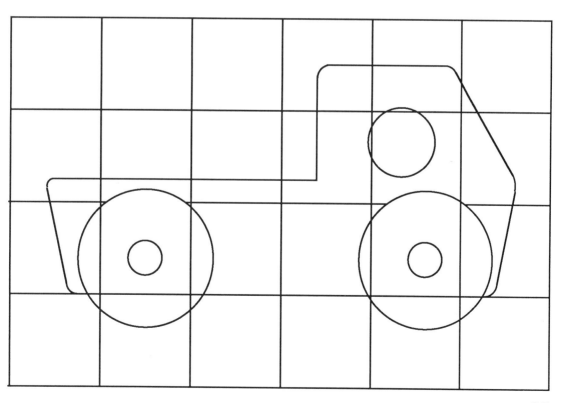

97

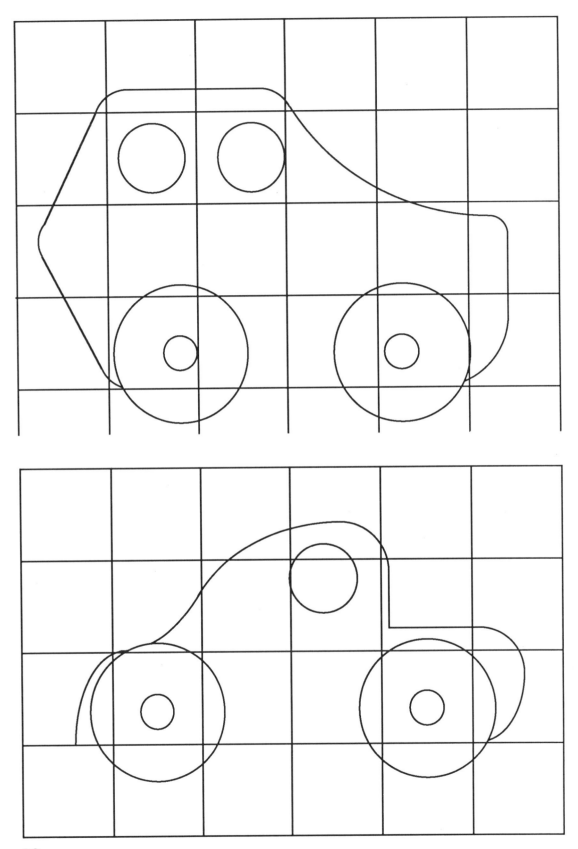

98

3
INTERMEDIATE-LEVEL PROJECTS

This section of patterns is designed to provide projects that are suited for someone who has some experience with the band saw. An ambitious beginner could also do these projects. All of these projects require more than one piece of wood. Many of the items have two sides that have an identical shape. These two pieces should be cut and sanded at the same time. Hold the pieces together using hot-melt glue, double-faced tape, or brads. This technique is faster than cutting each piece separately, and it assures that both pieces are exactly the same.

Some of the projects require that you make a dado to hold a shelf. All joinery should be done before the curves are cut because it is much easier to work with a board that has square corners and parallel sides.

Wall Box

This painted wall shelf is made of ¼-inch pine. The bottom is square but you could add an angle so that the sides spread outwards. The top design can be

Wall box.

simply circular or you can select one of the optional patterns. You can also make a new design using the three-inch by three-inch grid. The sides are laid out with a nine-inch square grid.

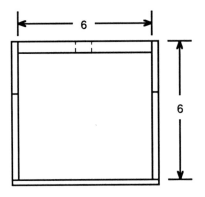

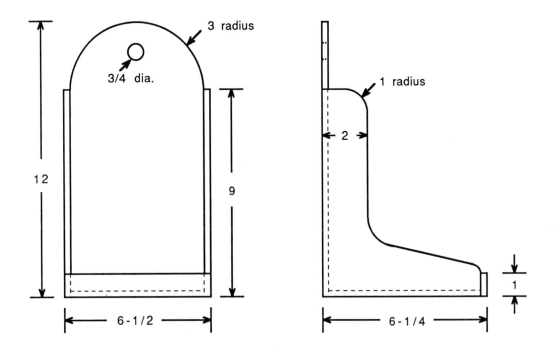

Plan for wall box.

Optional patterns for wall box top.

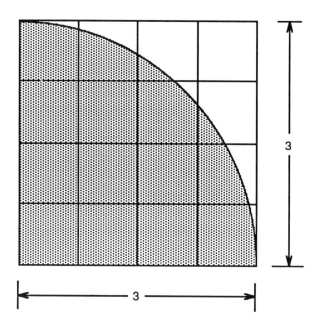

3

3

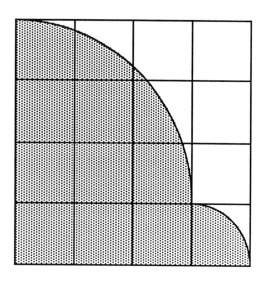

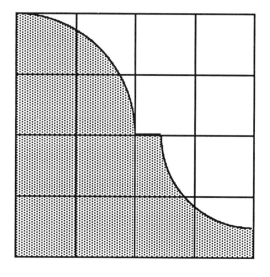

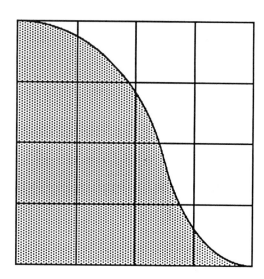

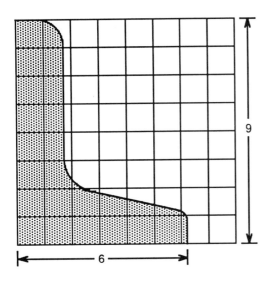

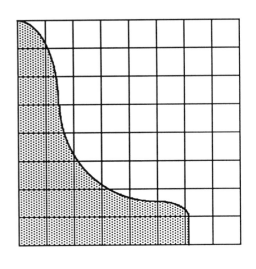

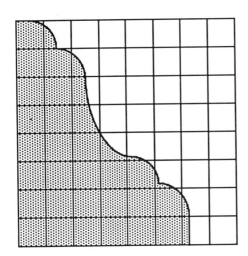

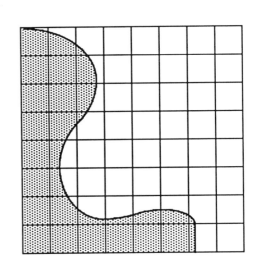

Optional patterns for wall box sides.

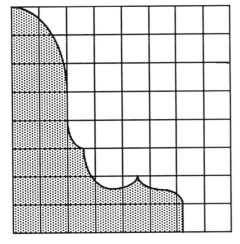

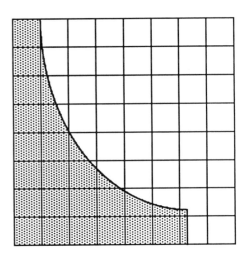

102

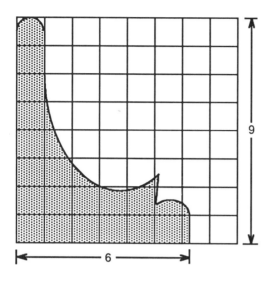
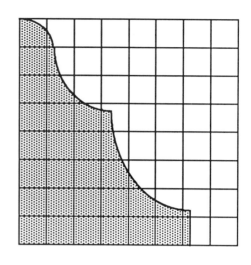

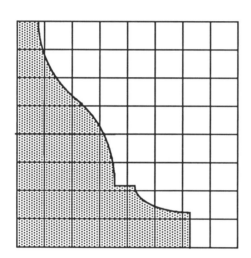
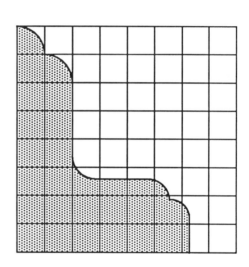

Optional patterns for wall box sides.

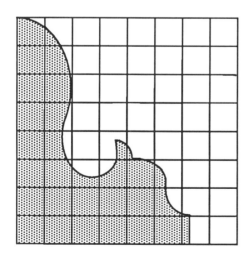
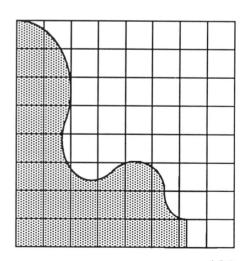

Shelf with Pegs

This shelf has a ledge and it has pegs for hanging clothes. This project is especially suitable for use in an entryway because it allows you to keep your outside gear in one place. Coats hang on the pegs and gloves and hats rest on the shelf. The shelf and the back are dadoed into the sides. This plan is shown to be 33 inches long but you can easily adjust the length to suit your space. For this project we recommend that you paint the final piece.

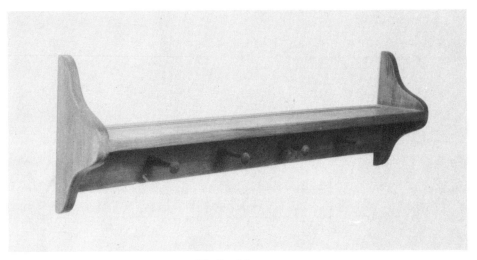

Shelf with pegs.

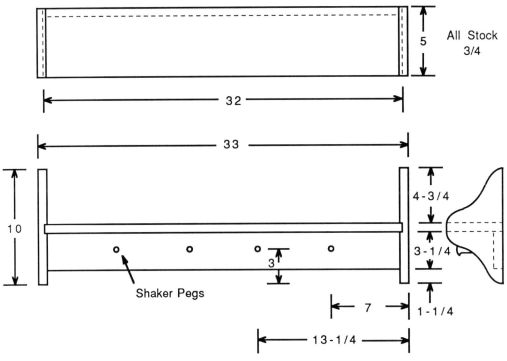

Plan for shelf with pegs.

Patterns for shelf side.

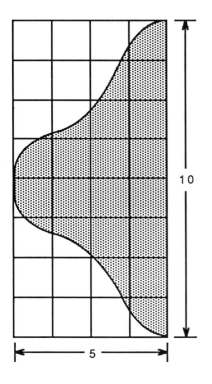

10

5

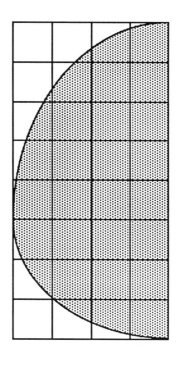

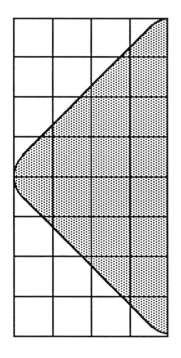

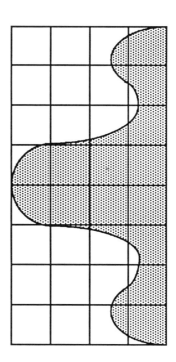

Patterns for shelf side.

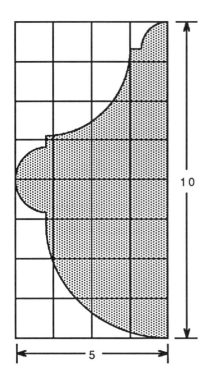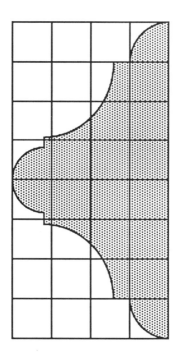

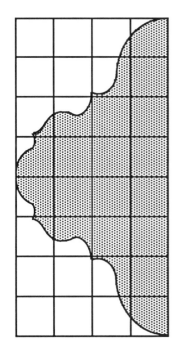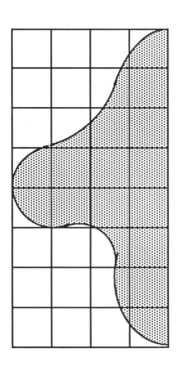

Corner Shelf

This corner shelf was originally designed and built in upstate New York in the 19th century. Its simple shape is very functional, although you could make it more decorative by using one of the optional patterns. The particular piece pictured is made of elm. All required stock is ¼-inch thick.

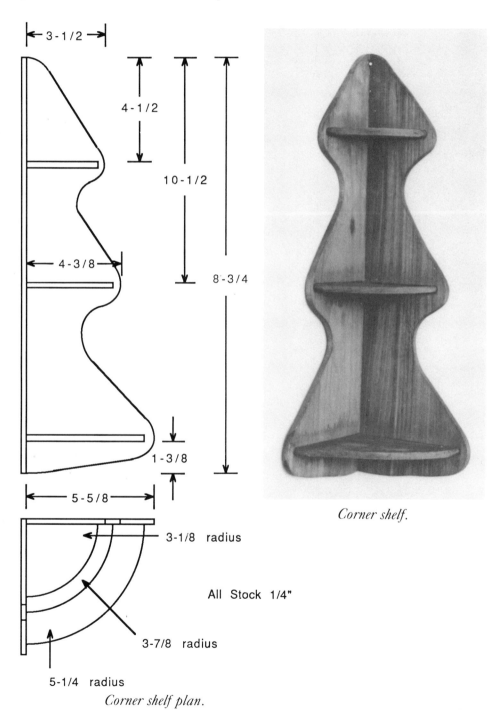

Corner shelf.

3-1/2

4-1/2

10-1/2

4-3/8

8-3/4

1-3/8

5-5/8

3-1/8 radius

All Stock 1/4"

3-7/8 radius

5-1/4 radius

Corner shelf plan.

Patterns for corner shelf.

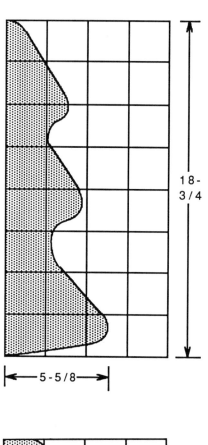

18-3/4

5-5/8

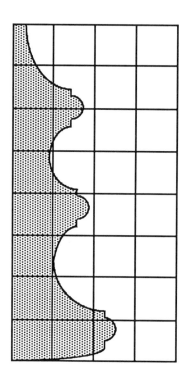

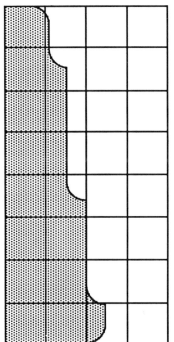

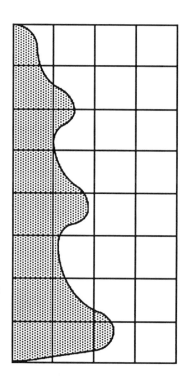

Decorative Shelf

This four-piece shelf is straightforward but has much charm. The shelf pictured is made of pine. The lower edge of the shelf top is routed with a decorative design. Nails and glue are used to hold the piece together, although you can choose the option of using screws and then plugging the holes with plugs of the same wood. The many optional patterns allow you to make this piece as simple or as decorative as you would like.

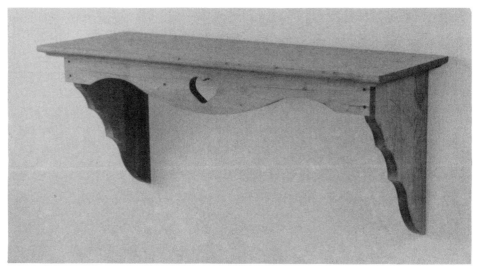

Decorative shelf.

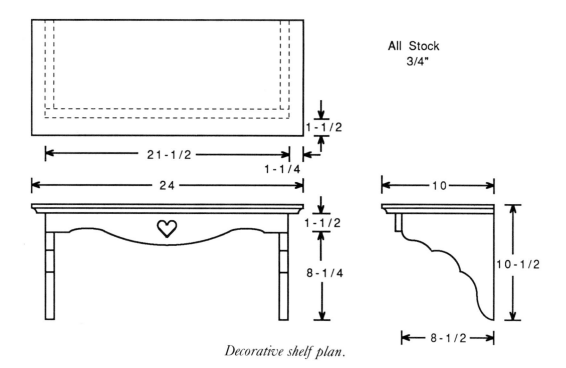

All Stock
3/4"

Decorative shelf plan.

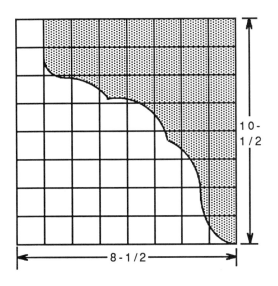

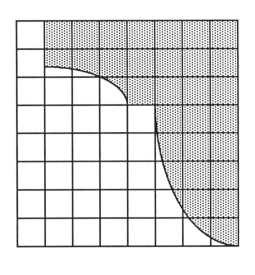

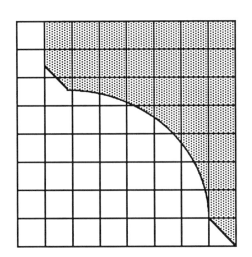

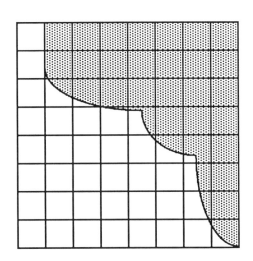

Patterns for decorative shelf side supports.

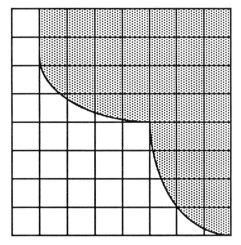

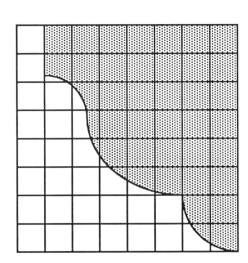

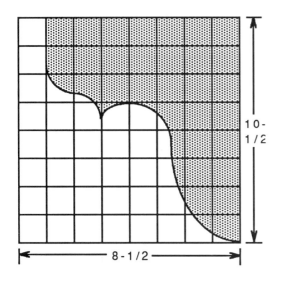

10-1/2

8-1/2

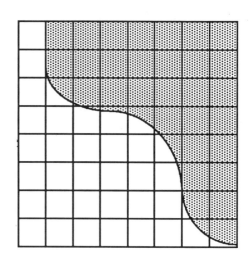

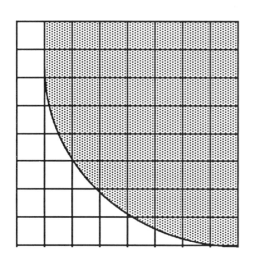

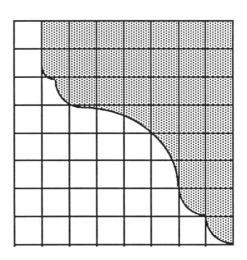

Patterns for decorative shelf side supports.

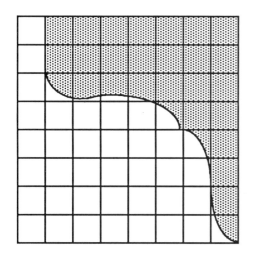

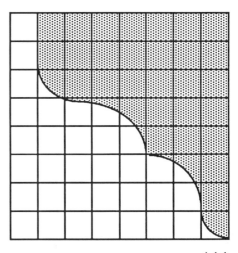

111

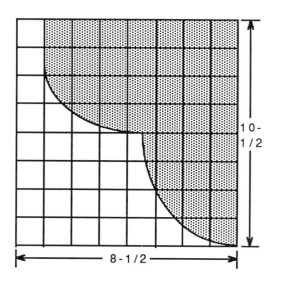

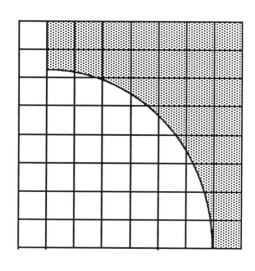

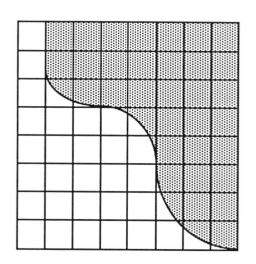

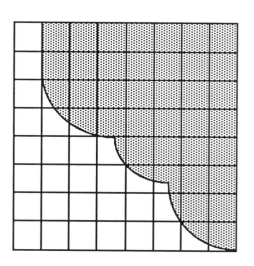

Patterns for decorative shelf side supports.

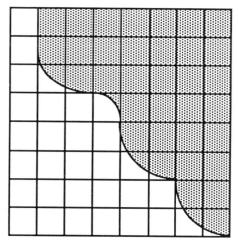

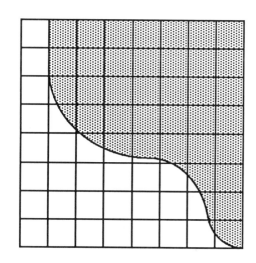

Half-patterns for decorative shelf front.

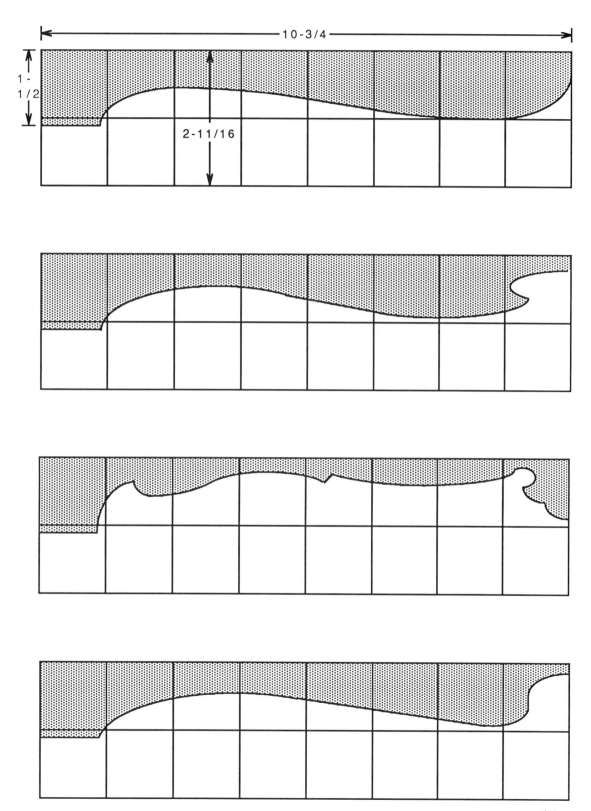

Half-patterns for decorative shelf front.

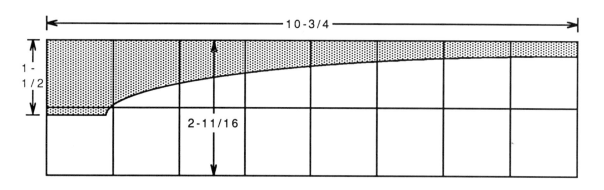

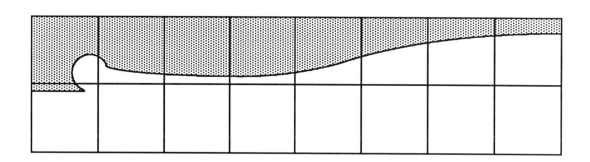

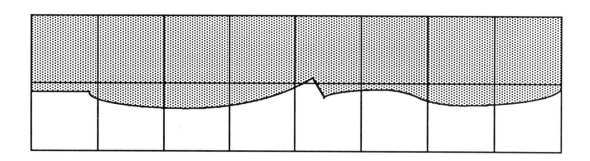

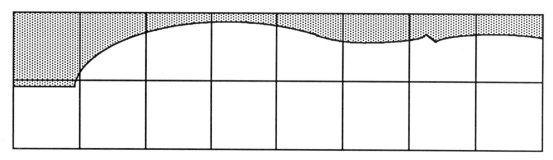

Half-patterns for decorative shelf front.

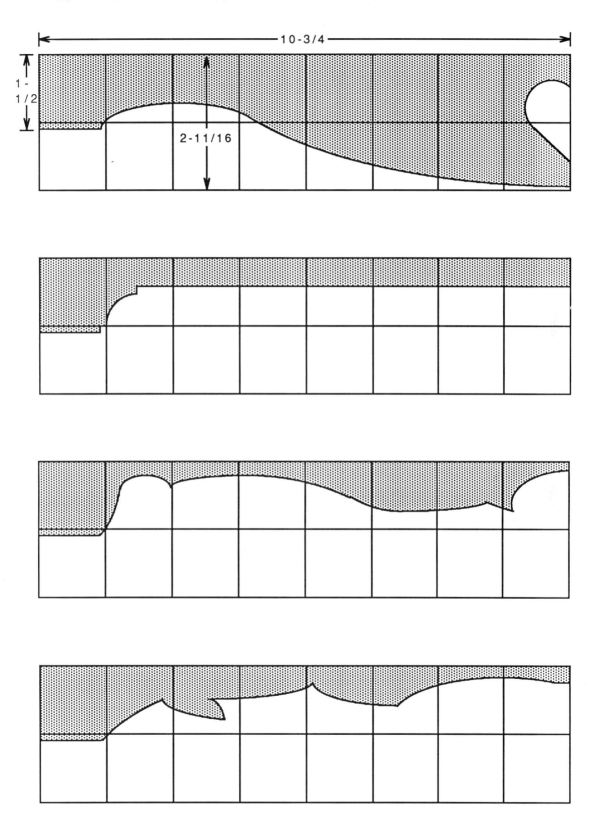

Message Center

Every household needs a place to collect and store information, notes, and lists. This design was originally a high school shop project. It includes a tablet, corkboard, a tray for pens or pencils, and hooks for keys. It would probably look even better in a darker wood such as cherry or walnut.

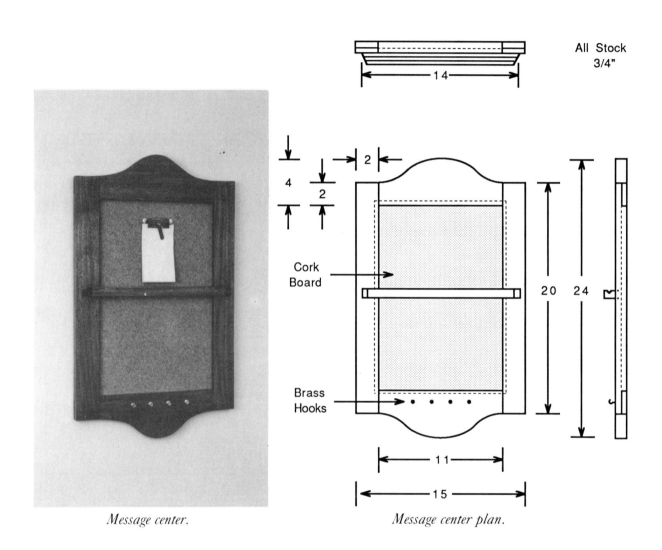

Message center.   *Message center plan.*

Message center half-patterns for top.

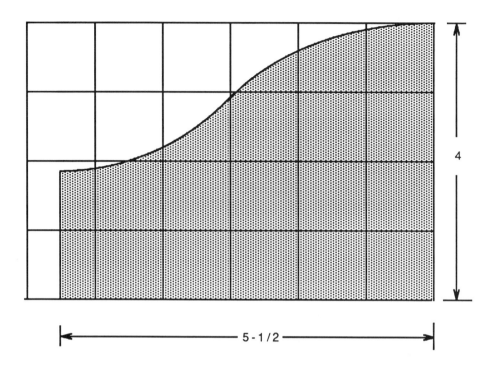

5 - 1 / 2

4

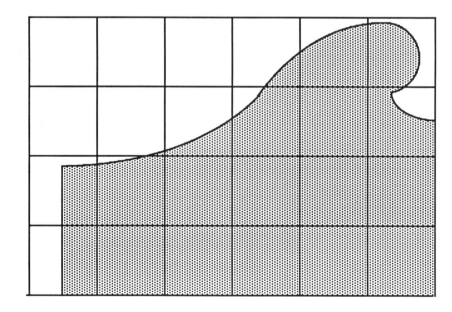

Small Early American Mirror

This small early American mirror has a simple elegance about it. The particular mirror pictured is made of pine and painted, although the design would also look good in most natural woods. The decorative top is added to a bottom frame that has mitred corners. You could also make the frame corners so that they are square rather than using a mitre. The frame is then rabbetted in the back to accept the glass mirror. There are a number of options for attaching the top to the frame such as dowels, biscuits, splines, tongue-and-groove, or screws.

Small early American mirror.

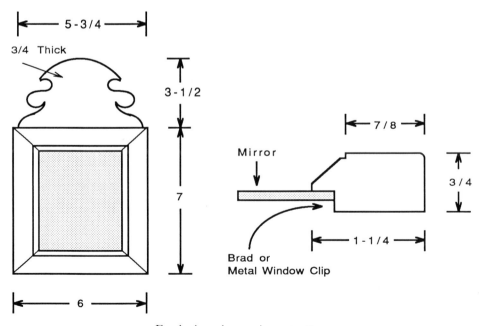

Early American mirror pattern.

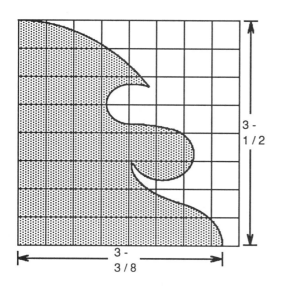

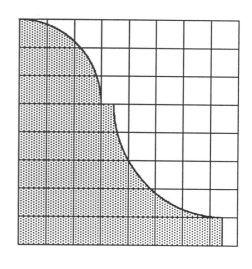

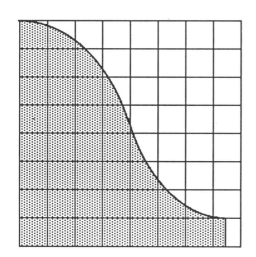

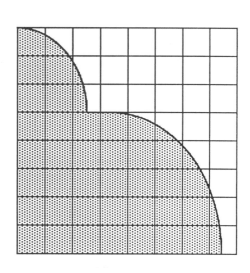

Half-patterns for mirror top.

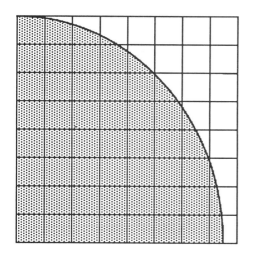

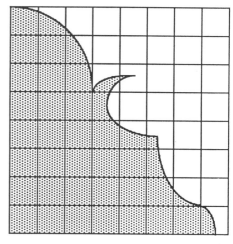

119

Small Bench

The small bench pictured is made of clear pine. You have the option of using nails or screws and plugs for the structural support. This bench is small but you can easily enlarge it by making a bigger grid for the end. The end is made using a half-pattern; the two halves are then glued together. We suggest that you cut the four halves of the sides at the same time to be most efficient.

Small bench.

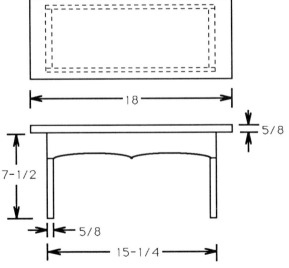

Small bench plan.

120

Half-patterns for bench end.

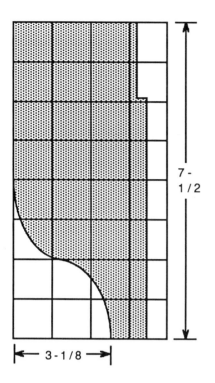

7 -
1 / 2

3 - 1 / 8

3 - 3 / 4

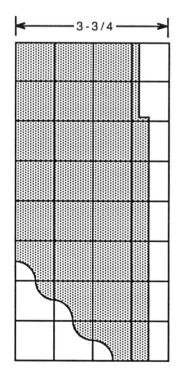

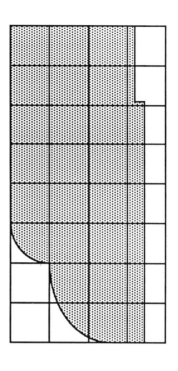

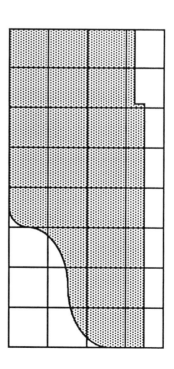

Half-patterns for bench end.

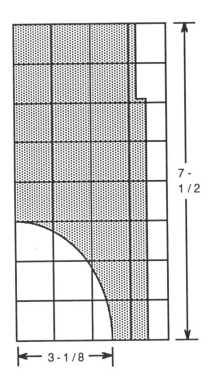

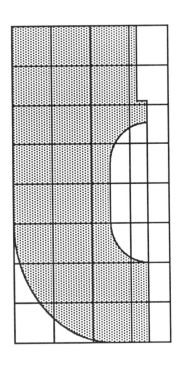

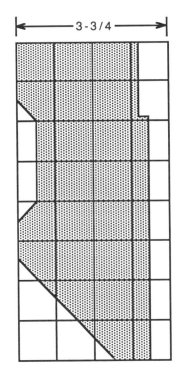

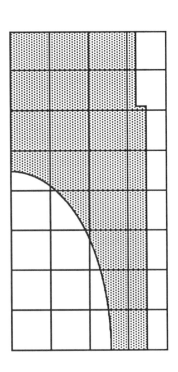

Small Table

The small table pictured has a painted bottom with a butternut top. The height of 24 inches can be adjusted to match a specific need. This design would make a good lamp, end, or side table. The legs can be plain or they can be made more decorative by routing or shaping a design. Although this design is essentially square, you can easily stretch the patterns as described earlier to make the table rectangular.

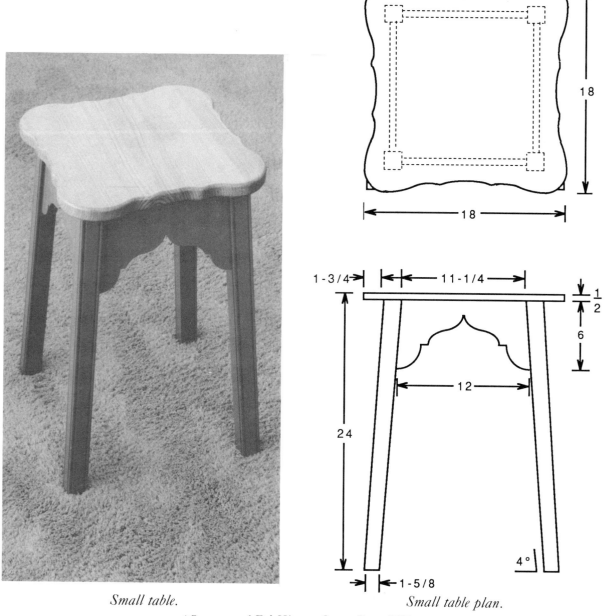

Small table.

Small table plan.

(Courtesy of Ed Hinsa, Green Bay, WI)

123

Quarter-patterns of small tabletop.
Each grid pattern is 9 inches square.

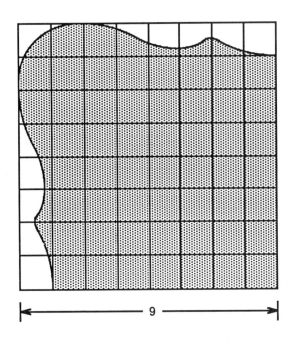

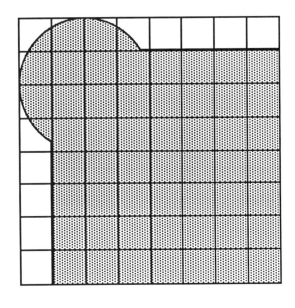

9

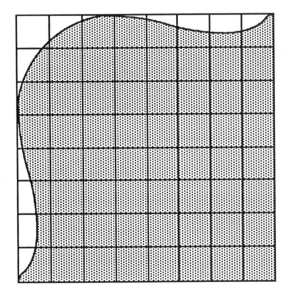

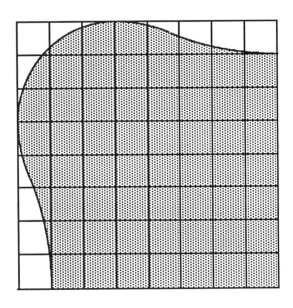

Half-patterns for small table apron.

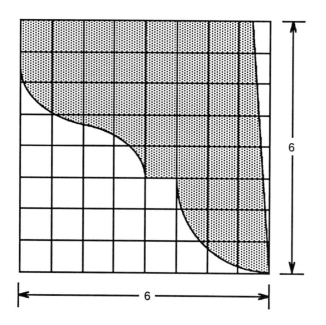

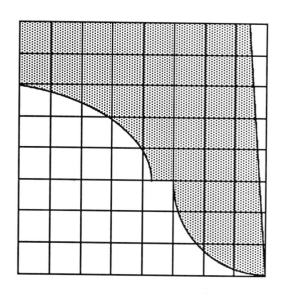

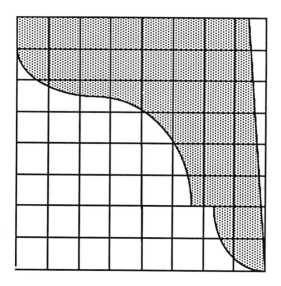

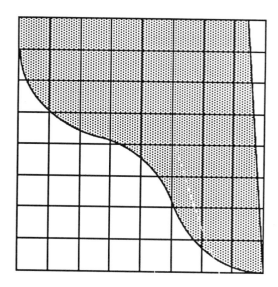

Decorative Door

A decorative door can add greatly to the character of a piece of furniture or a cabinet. This door top and panel were both made using the pattern-sawing technique described earlier in chapter one. After the waste is removed with the band saw, the edge is trimmed with a flush-cutting router bit.

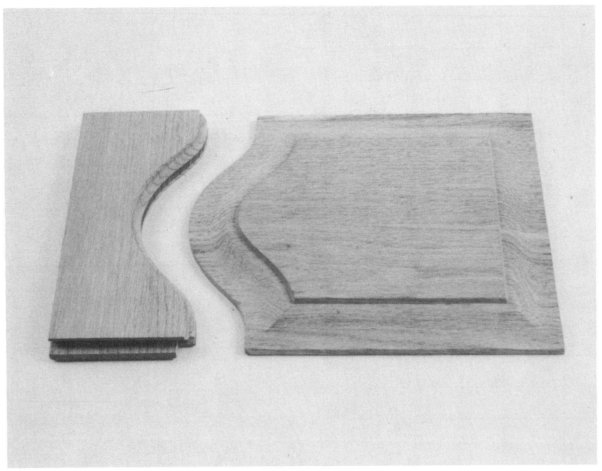

Decorative door.

Half-patterns for decorative door.

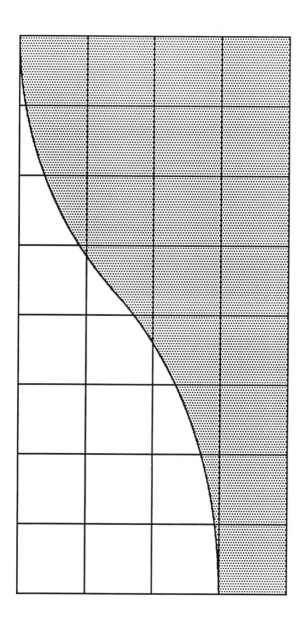
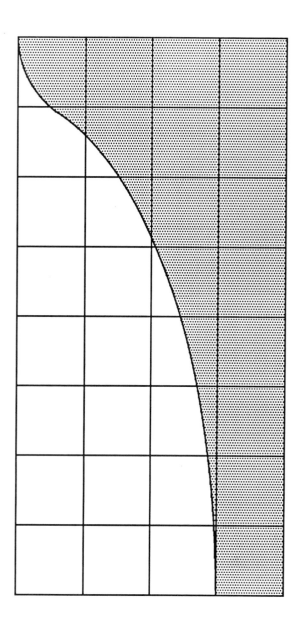

Half-patterns for decorative door.

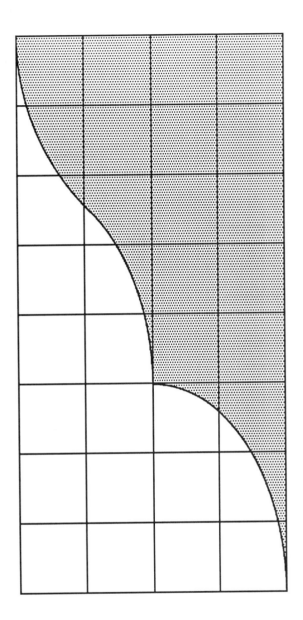
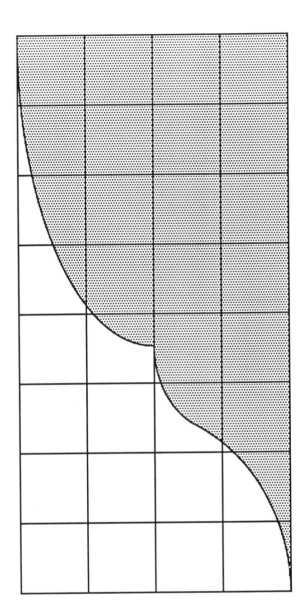

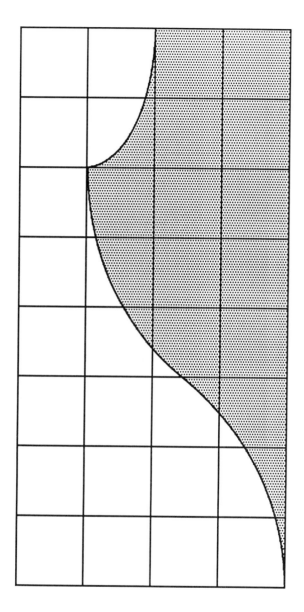

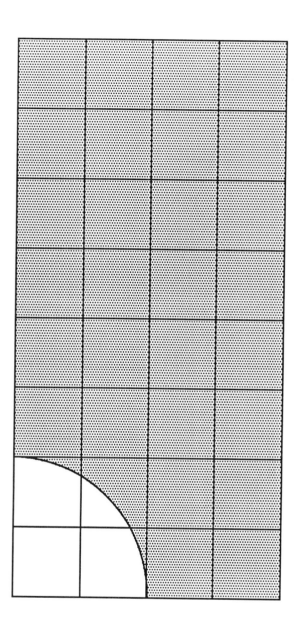

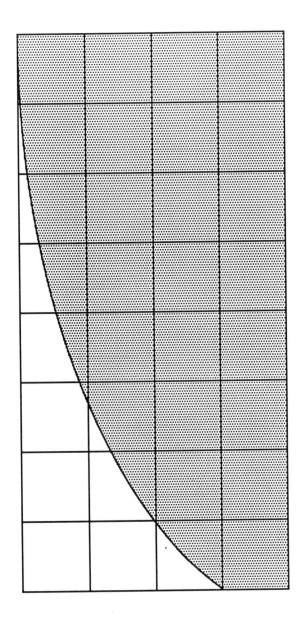
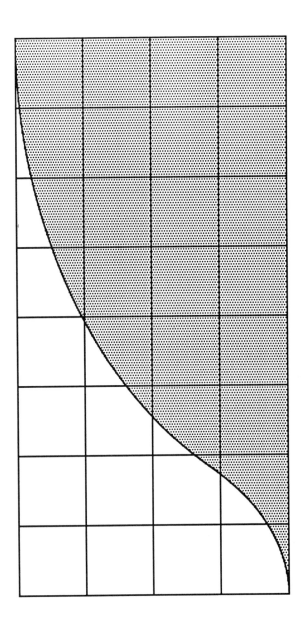

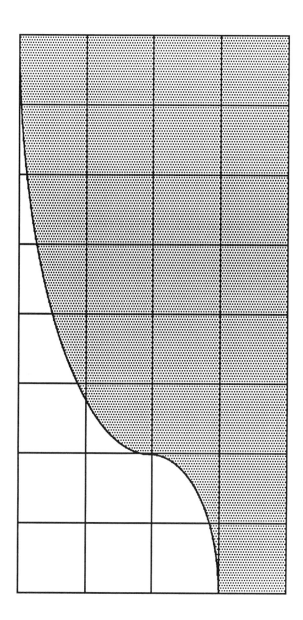 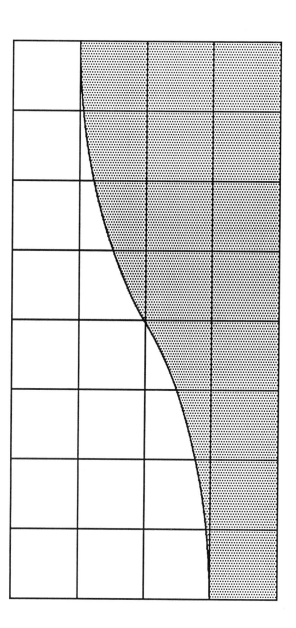

Pipe Box

The pipe box is a remnant from the past when long-stemmed pipes were in fashion. The design can function today as a container such as a letter holder. The drawer can be used to hold stamps and labels. The piece pictured is made of ⅜-inch cherry and is finished with a clear oil. The back is made using a half-pattern. The sides should be cut and sanded at the same time.

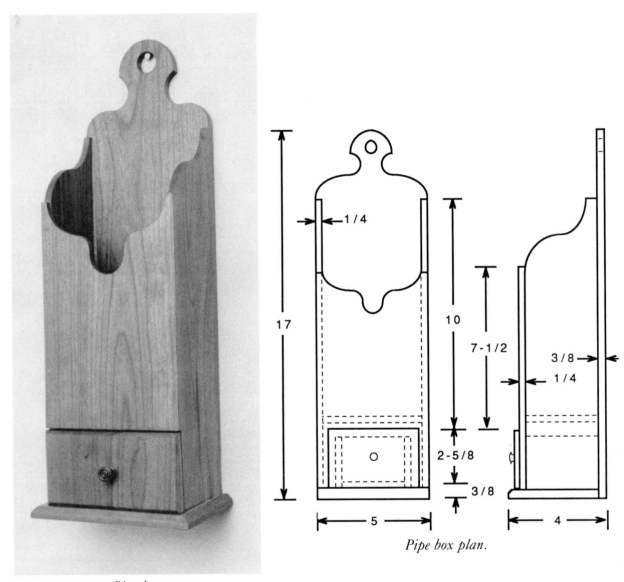

Pipe box.

Pipe box plan.

Half-patterns for pipe box.

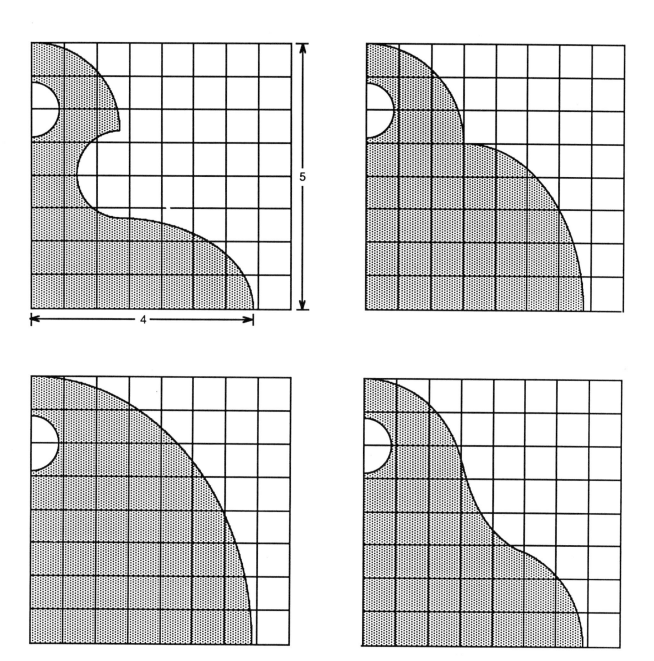

Patterns for the front and side of pipe box.

Front

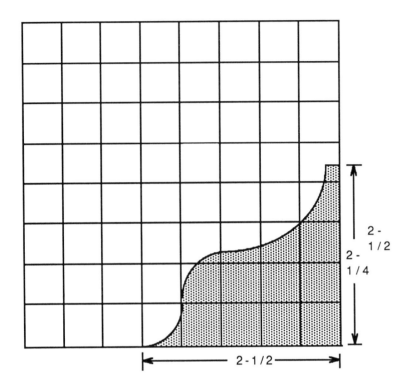

Side

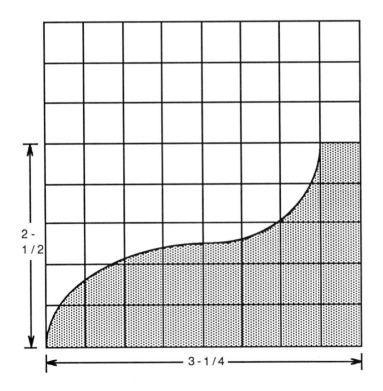

Band Saw Boxes

Band saw boxes are made in every conceivable shape and style. Here we provide the plans and techniques for making several different designs. Two options for boxes that are particularly suitable for executing on the band saw are pictured below.

Band saw boxes.

The design for the box on the left is based on the recognizable shape of a maple leaf. The box on the right is a free-form design. The maple leaf box has a removable lid. The free-form box is held together by a key. After the key is removed, the top is slid off to expose the inside of the box.

Also included in this section on band saw boxes are a glove box, a plain box with decorative feet, and a box with a sliding cover.

The maple leaf box has a removable lid.

The key must be pulled out before the lid will slide out.

To make the maple leaf box, mark the pattern on the top of the workpiece. Cut out the outline and then saw the top off. Cut out the inside plug by entering from the stem area of the leaf. You will need to cut two pieces off the plug. Cut one off each side of the plug and label each with a letter. The piece

Draw the pattern on the top of the box or attach a paper pattern with either tape or rubber cement.

Cut the outline of the box and then cut the top off, being careful to position the stock so that the gain is parallel with the blade. This will produce the best finish. A ⅛-inch blade with 14 teeth per inch (TPI) is used for this operation.

Cut the inside plug by entering through the stem area of the leaf.

cut off the bottom of the plug should be the bottom of the box, so mark it B. The piece cut off the top of the plug will be attached to the top later and should be labelled T.

To mark the correct position of the lid base, place the body over the top piece and use a pencil to mark the inside cutout on the top piece. Tap in two brads that will later be used to locate the top on the base.

Cut a piece off the top and the bottom of the plug. One piece will be the bottom of the box and the other piece will be the base of the top.

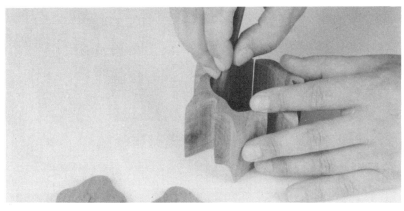

To mark the position of the top base, place the body on the top and mark the inside.

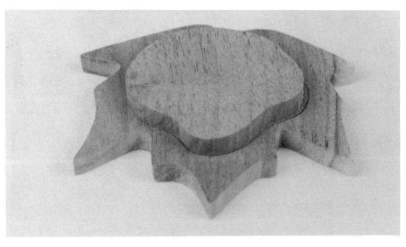

The pencil line marks the correct location of the top base.

137

Next, glue the body together in the area of the stem. Gap-filling glue is best for this. At the same time, glue the bottom piece in place. While these are drying, finish the underside of the top, the top base, and the edge of the top with a spray-on-suede lining.

After the top oil finish dries, glue the base to the top. The brads should extend only about one sixteenth of an inch from the base. The brads help to locate the top exactly. Finally, finish the bottom of the cover base as well as the inside and bottom of the box with the spray-on-suede lining.

The body seam is then glued together.

Glue the base and the top together using the brads to locate the exact position of the base and to keep the base from moving. The brads extend through the base and into the top about a sixteenth of an inch.

Here the bottom is shown glued in place using gap-filling glue. Wait for the body seam and the bottom glue to dry before finishing the inside.

138

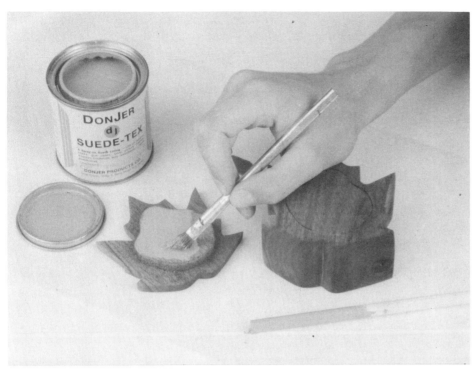

The inside of the box is then finished with spray-on suede; the adhesive for the finish is applied with a brush.

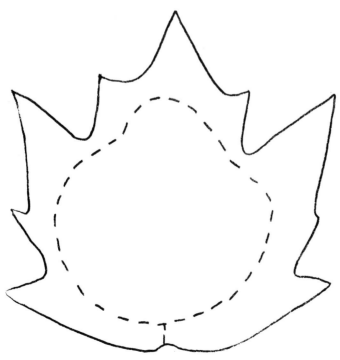

Maple leaf box pattern.

Several optional patterns for a leaf box design are provided, if you would prefer to make the box in a design other than, or in addition to, the maple leaf design.

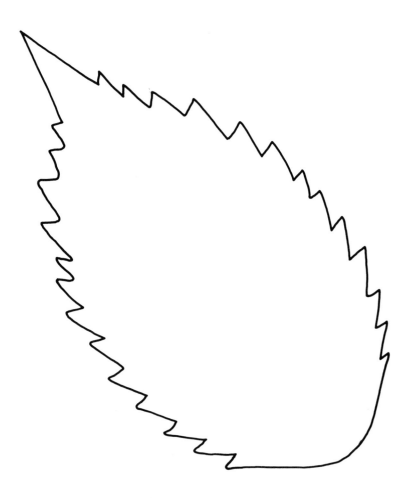

141

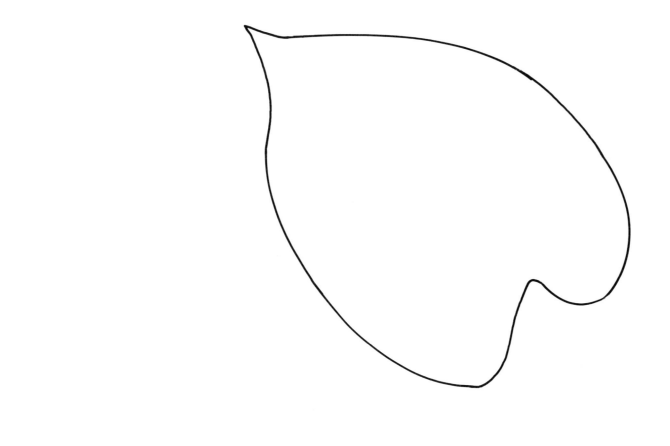

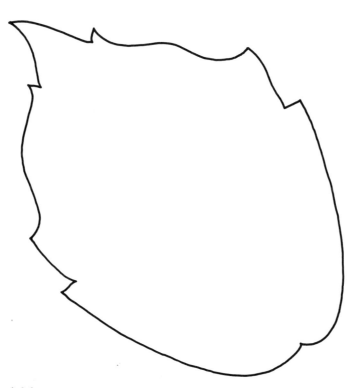

144

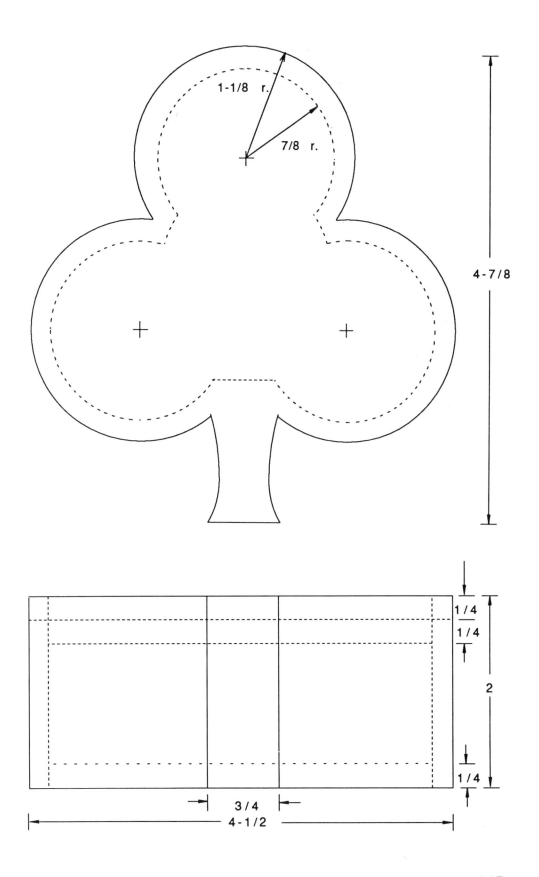

1-1/8 r.

7/8 r.

4-7/8

1/4
1/4
2
1/4

3/4

4-1/2

145

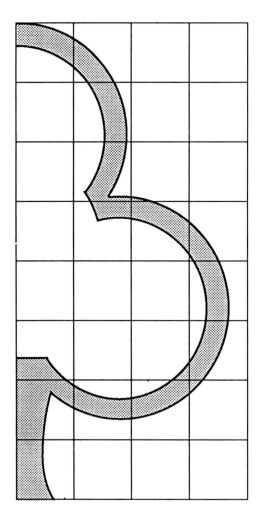

*Cloverleaf box
half-pattern.*

146

Glove box, made from pine.

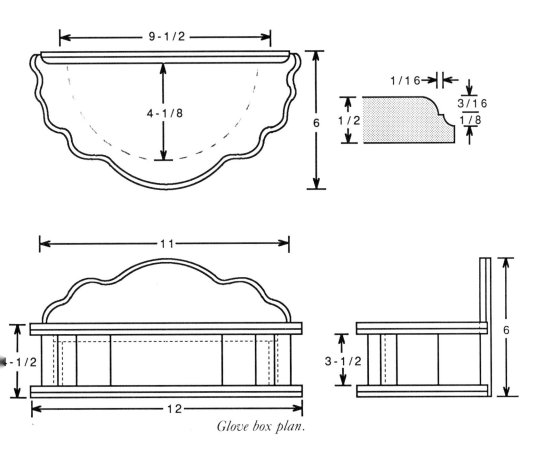

Glove box plan.

147

Half-pattern for glove box.

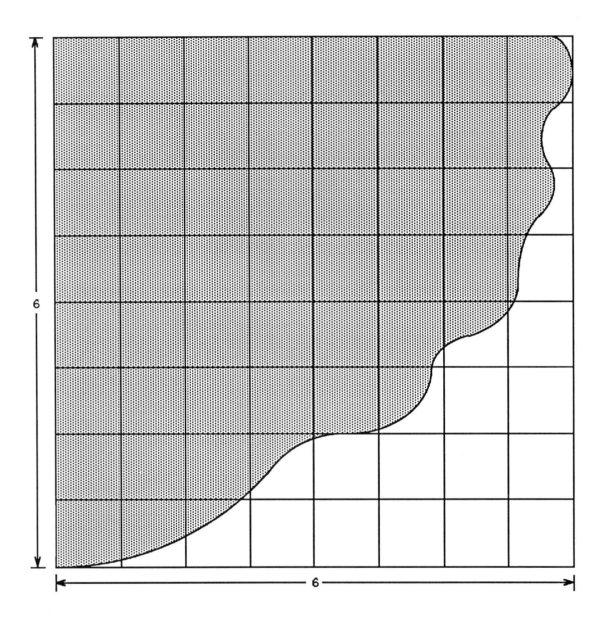

Plain box with decorative feet. (Courtesy of Andrew Gilderson)

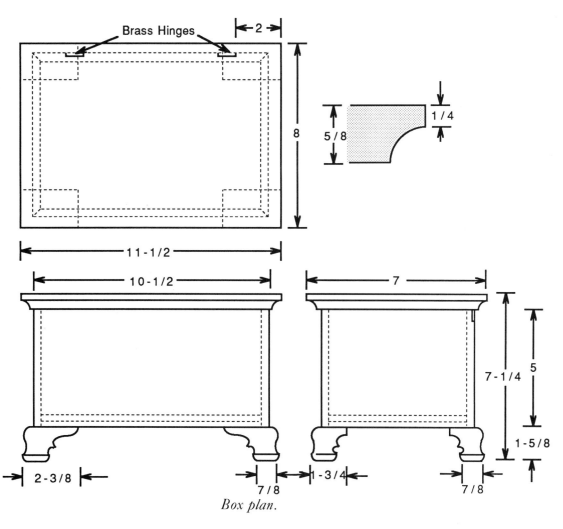

Box plan.

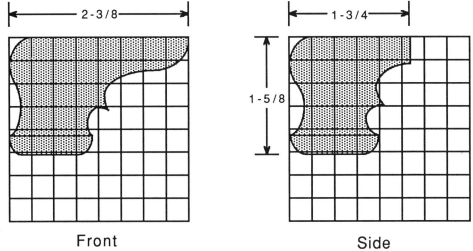

2-3/8

1-3/4

1-5/8

Front   Side

Detail of decorative foot for plain box.

Box with sliding cover.

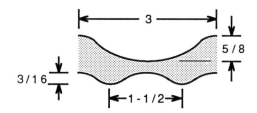

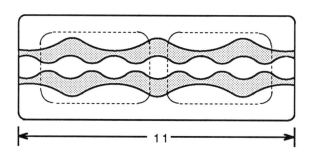

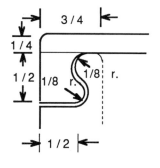

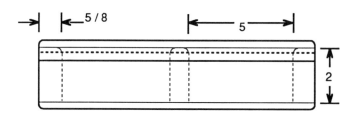

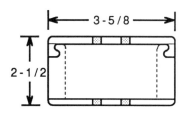

Box with sliding cover plan.

Tapered-Leg Table

This table is based on Shaker furniture design. The Shakers were known for their simple and practical designs. You can make this table more decorative by using one of the optional apron designs. The tabletop is rectangular but you can add a decorative edge. You may want to consider one of the optional designs for the top of the small table shown earlier.

You also have the option of using a plain leg or you can use a one-, two- or four-sided taper. The leg taper is done on the band saw using a taper jig. The best way to join the leg to the apron is to use a mortise-and-tenon joint. Note that the tenon is made before the apron design is cut out.

Tapered-leg table.

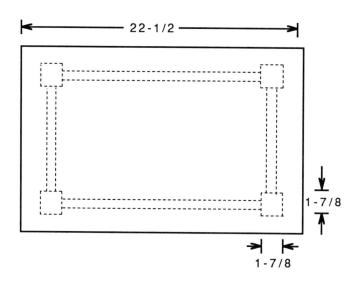

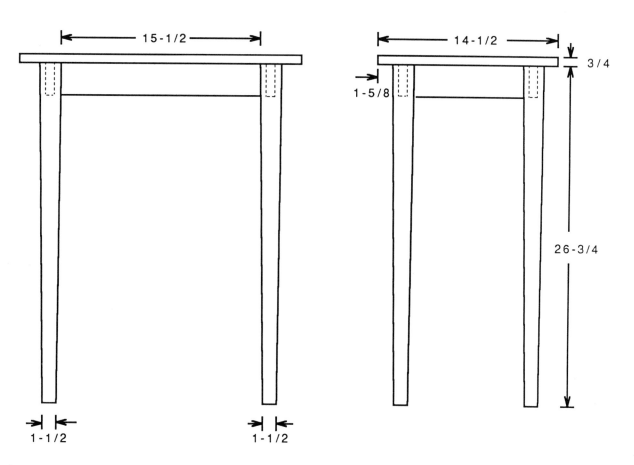

Tapered-leg table plan.

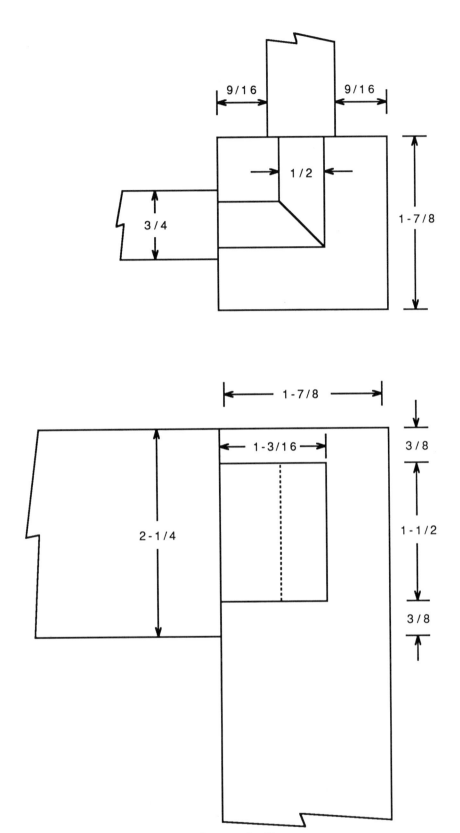

Mortise-and-tenon detail.

154

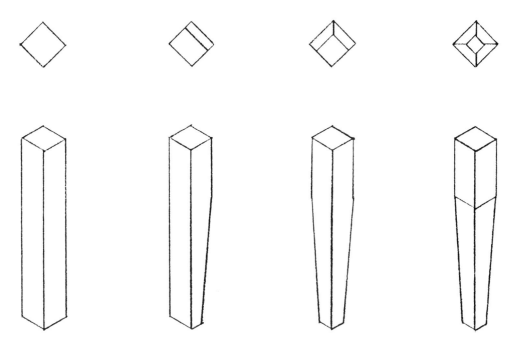

As an option to the full tapered leg, a leg can be tapered on only one or two sides or left untapered.

The step jig is used for adjacent- or opposite-side tapers.

Half-patterns for table apron.

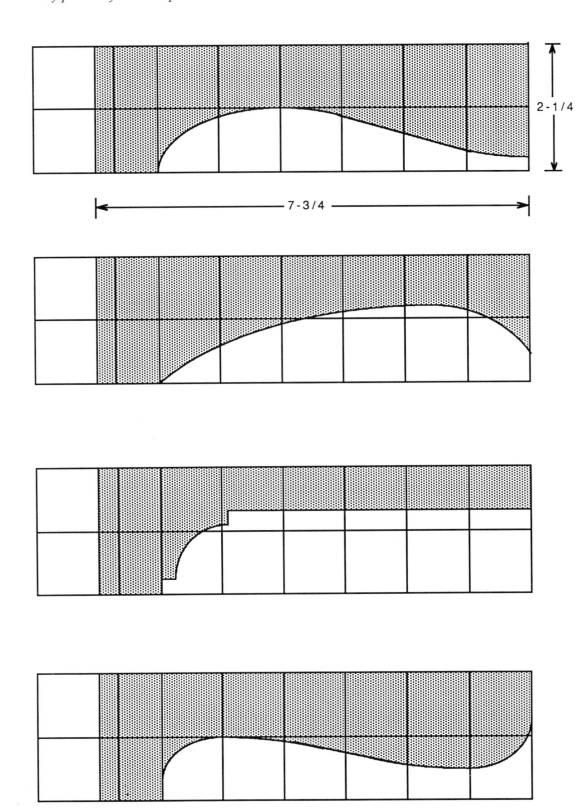

4
ADVANCED BAND SAW PROJECTS

These projects are made using techniques that require some experience with the band saw. It may be appropriate that you practice with scrap wood before attempting some of these techniques with full-size pieces. For more background and to develop your skill and confidence, we suggest you consult our two earlier band saw books which are described in the introduction.

Decorative Corner Shelf

This decorative corner shelf is a challenging project because the aprons below the top and bottom shelf need to be cut in a circular shape. The quarter-circle

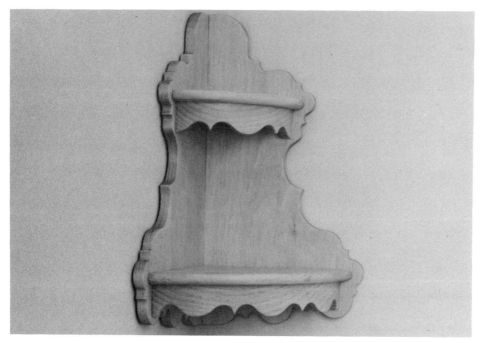

Decorative corner shelf, made of white pine.

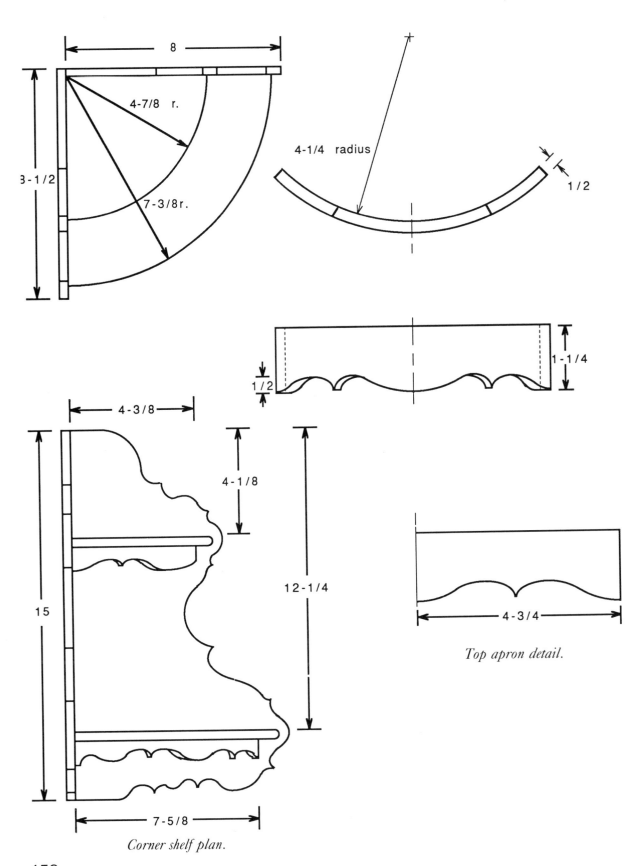

8

4-7/8 r.

3-1/2

7-3/8 r.

4-1/4 radius

1/2

1-1/4

1/2

4-3/8

4-1/8

12-1/4

15

7-5/8

Corner shelf plan.

4-3/4

Top apron detail.

decorative pattern is then cut with the outside curve resting on the saw table. When making this cut the pattern is attached to the inside of the curved apron with rubber cement or removable spray-mount adhesive. As with the other projects, cut the dadoes before making the decorative cuts.

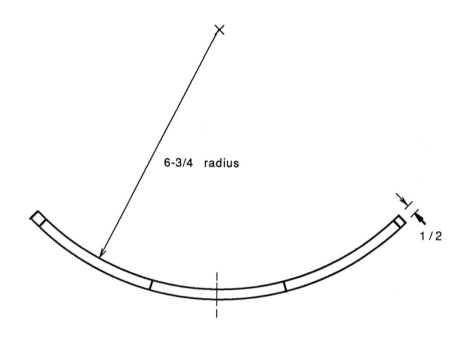

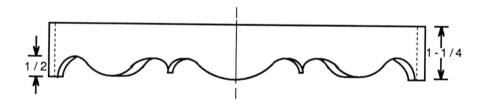

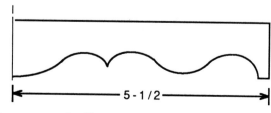

Bottom apron detail.

159

Patterns for corner shelf.

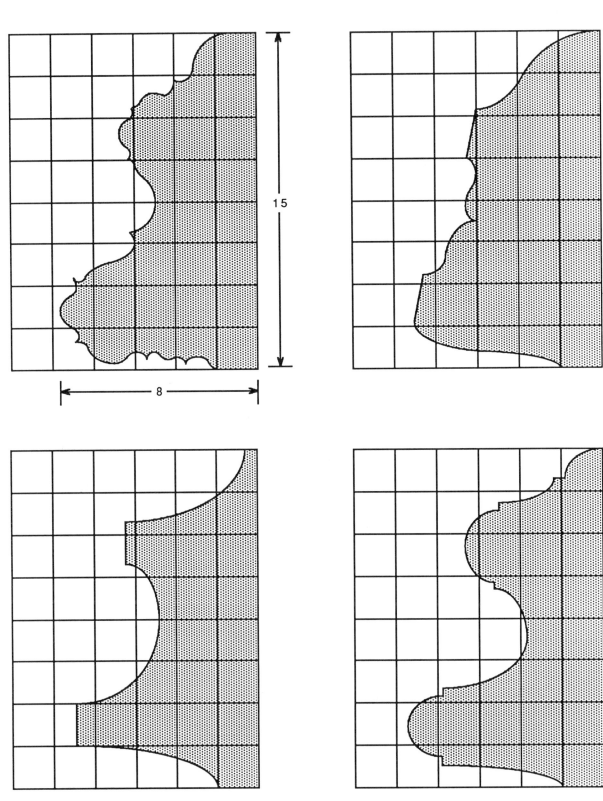

15

8

Chippendale Mirror

This mirror is designed in the Chippendale style. The mirror pictured is made in walnut. The frame is shaped and then the corners are mitred. The decorative fretwork can be attached in a number of ways, such as using a dado or brads. The decorative pieces are all made from ¼-inch stock. Half-patterns are used to make this mirror.

Chippendale mirror.

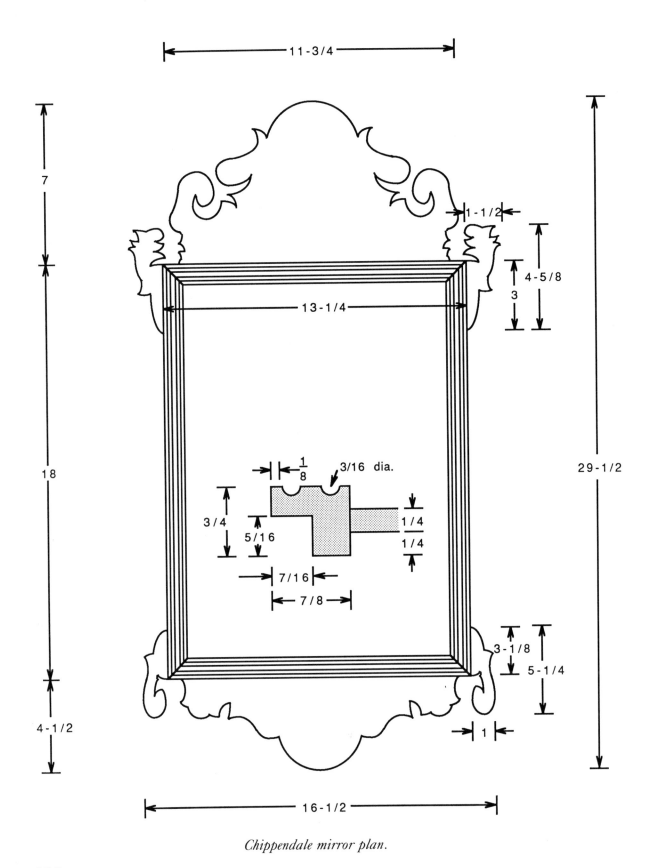

Chippendale mirror plan.

Half-pattern for mirror top.

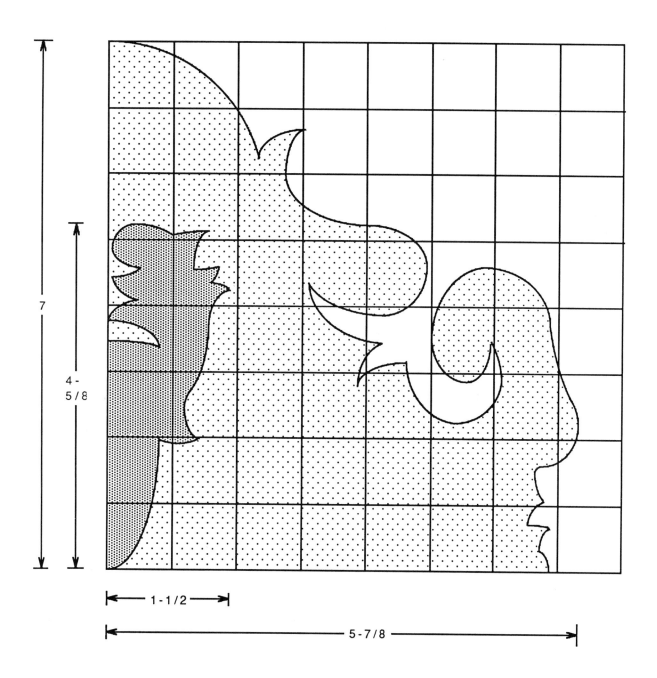

7

4 - 5 / 8

1 - 1 / 2

5 - 7 / 8

Half-pattern for mirror bottom.

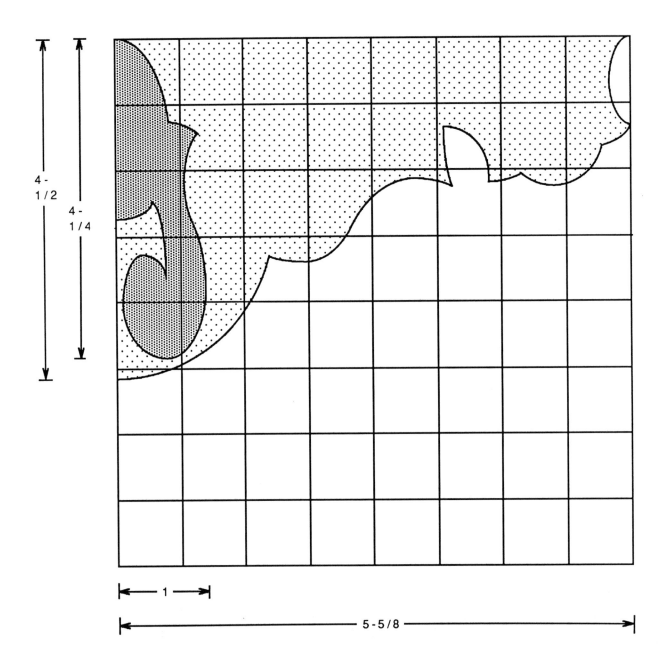

4 -
1 / 2

4 -
1 / 4

1

5 - 5 / 8

Queen Anne Footstool

This footstool is a project that requires care when making the legs and also when joining the legs to the stretcher. The seat is solid wood with a foam rubber pad. It is best to make the joints before cutting the cabriole leg.

Queen Anne footstool.

16

2-3/4

Cabriole leg patterns.

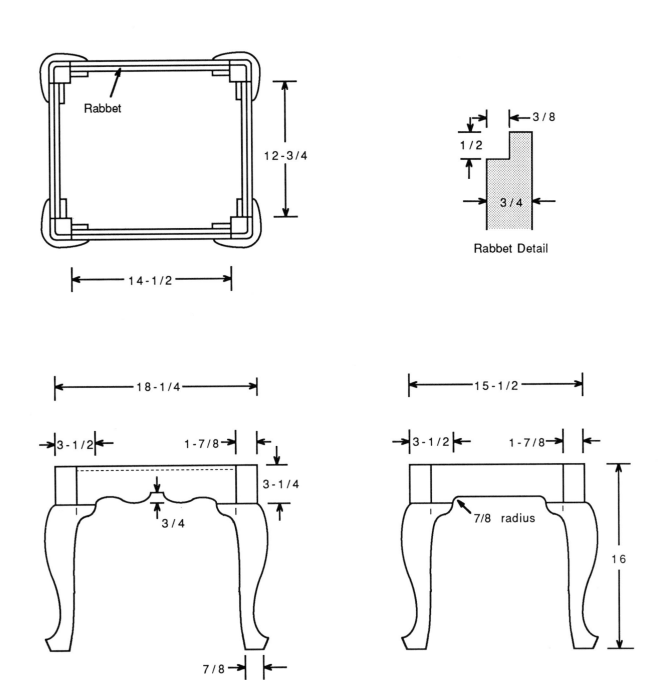

Rabbet

12-3/4

14-1/2

3/8

1/2

3/4

Rabbet Detail

18-1/4

3-1/2

1-7/8

3-1/4

3/4

7/8

15-1/2

3-1/2

1-7/8

7/8 radius

16

Queen Anne footstool plan.

Multiple Shelf Unit

This multiple shelf unit is designed to hold a number of small items. The unit pictured is made from cherry and displays an egg cup collection. It is important that you make the dadoes or dovetails that hold the piece together before making the decorative cuts.

Multiple shelf unit, made from cherry. (Courtesy of David Morris, Austin, TX)

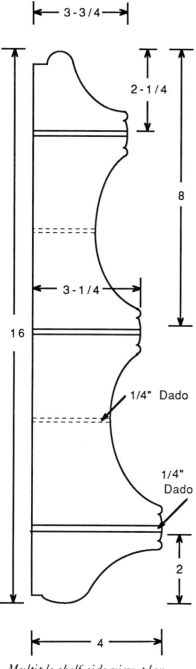

Multiple shelf side view plan.

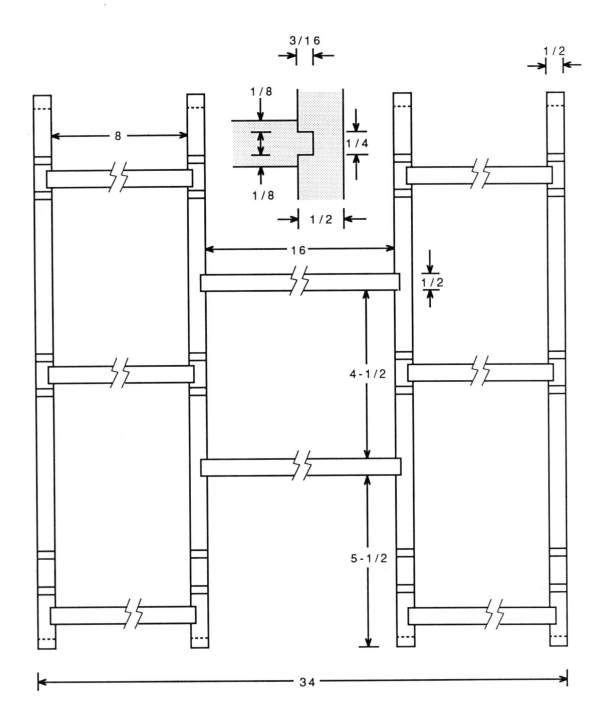

Multiple shelf plan.

Multiple shelf patterns.

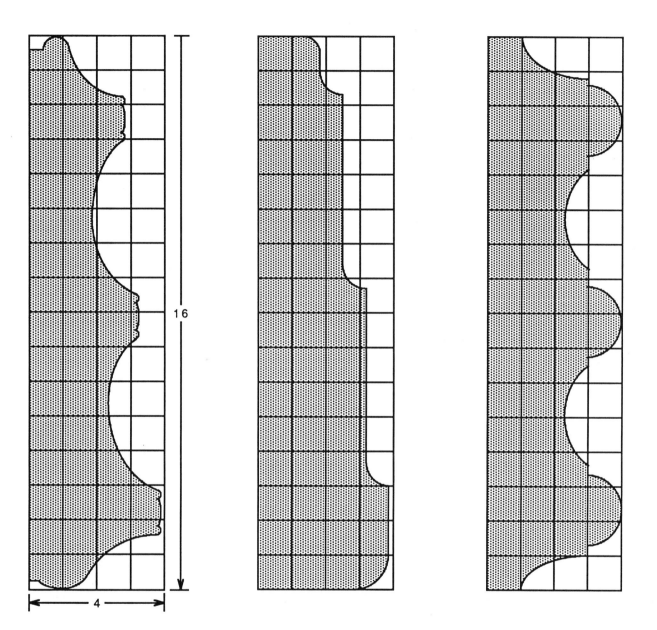

Intarsia

Different colored woods are often used next to each other for a decorative effect or design. When veneer is used it is referred to as *marquetry;* when solid wood is used it is called *intarsia*. The wildlife scene in wood is an example of well executed intarsia. It is best to use a ¹⁄₁₆-inch blade when doing this kind of fine work.

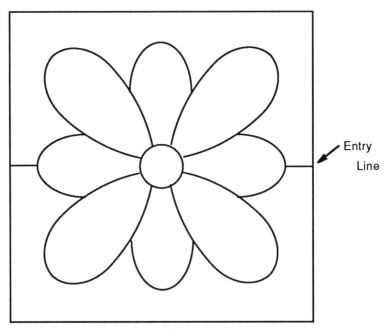

Wildlife design intarsia—solid wood, rather than veneer, is used.
(Made by Glenn Elvig, Minneapolis, MN)

170

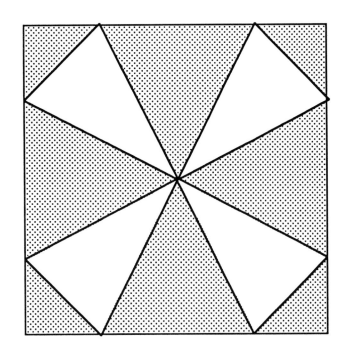

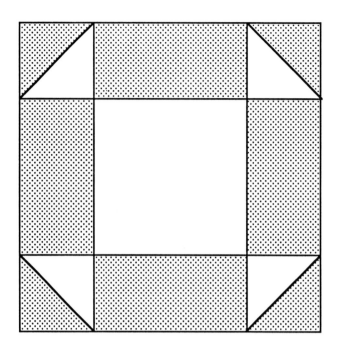

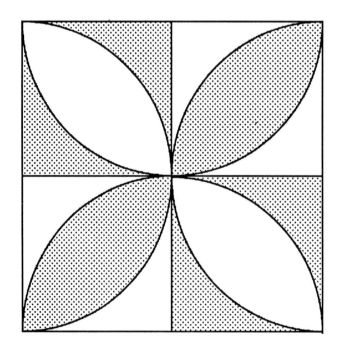

173

174

175

Projects Using the Cut-and-Glue Technique

The band saw cannot be used (without welding) in the same manner as the scroll saw to make interior cuts. The scroll saw blade can be disconnected and reconnected inside a hole, thus allowing a true inside cut. However, the band saw can also be used to make "inside" cuts by cutting two pieces and gluing them together with what is called the cut-and-glue technique. The technique used on the band saw is simply to cut the pattern in the two halves at the same time, and then glue the pieces together to create the design.

The interior cut can be either decorative or functional such as for a picture frame. If you made any of the frames in chapter two, then you have already used a simple version of this technique.

Ideally the piece should be resawed so that when you glue the pieces back together they will match exactly. Cutting a single original board into two pieces while the original board is on edge is called *resawing*. Gluing the resawed pieces back together after the "inside" cuts have been made is called *bookmatching*. After the pieces are planed, they are held together with double-faced tape, hot-melt glue, or brads.

These items were made using a half-pattern and the cut-and-glue technique.

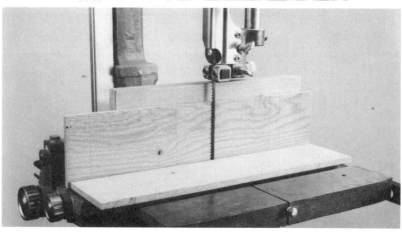

Although you can use the cut-and-glue technique with any two boards, the finished product will look better if the pieces are cut from the same board and glued back together.

The pattern is either taped to the boards or attached to the pieces using rubber cement. It is helpful to use drill holes to allow the piece to be turned easily for small details. The waste is then removed with a small band saw blade. The two halves are then glued back together. For narrow pieces joining inside the pattern, clothespins make good clamps for proper gluing.

Even though the scroll saw can be used to make a true interior cut, the cut-and-glue technique has several advantages. Both sides of the pattern are cut simultaneously which saves time, and both pieces are truly identical, improving the quality.

These pieces have been planed and are being prepared to be held together with double-faced tape.

The pattern has been attached to the pieces using rubber cement. Drill holes are used to facilitate cutting the pattern.

The largest piece of waste is removed. The 1/8-inch blade is used for this project.

The two halves have been completed. The pattern is removed and the pieces are then glued together.

177

Adjustable letter holder.

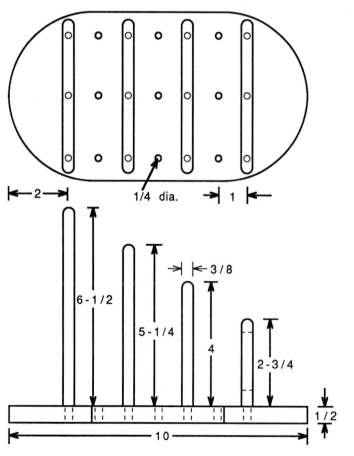

1/4 dia.

2

1

6 - 1/2

5 - 1/4

4

2 - 3/4

3/8

1/2

10

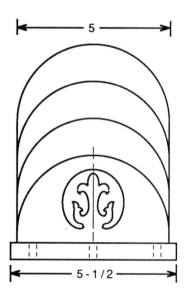

5

5 - 1/2

Letter holder plan.

178

Pencil Holder

The pencil holder is an example of a project using the cut-and-glue technique. The two matching halves that create the design are actually the decorative motif. This decoration, about ¼-inch thick, is glued to the front of a solid block that is two-inches thick. After the glue has dried, the holes that accept the pencils are drilled. Next, the corners are rounded using the band saw to remove the waste. The last step is to use a router with a round-over bit to create a rounded edge on the top and the holes.

Following the half-pattern that was used in making the pencil holder, the adjustable bookshelf, the letter holder, and the knockdown bookshelf are several optional half-patterns, one or more of which you may prefer using for these projects.

Pencil holder.

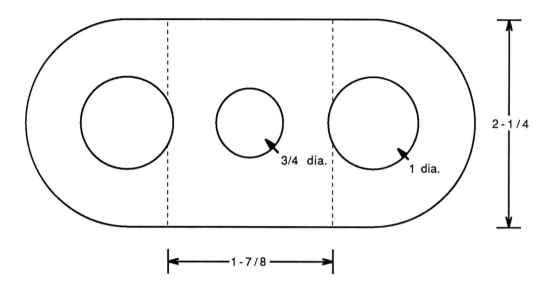

3/4 dia.

1 dia.

2-1/4

1-7/8

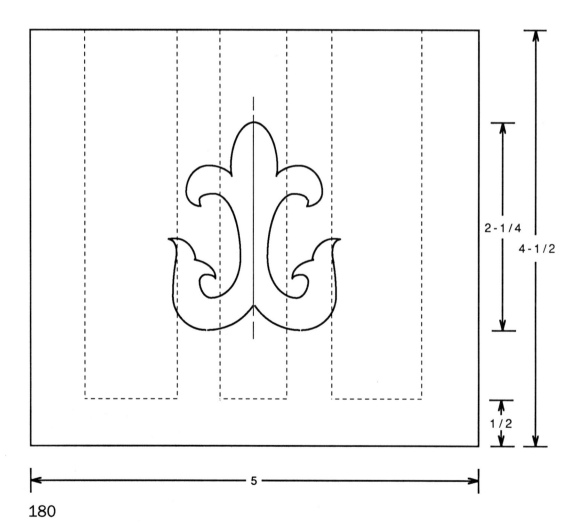

2-1/4

4-1/2

1/2

5

180

Adjustable bookshelf.

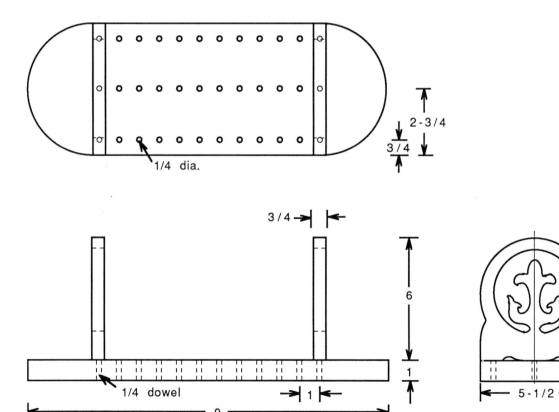

2 - 3 / 4

3 / 4

1/4 dia.

3 / 4

6

1

1/4 dowel

1

9

Adjustable bookshelf plan.

7

5 - 1 / 2

Knockdown bookshelf.

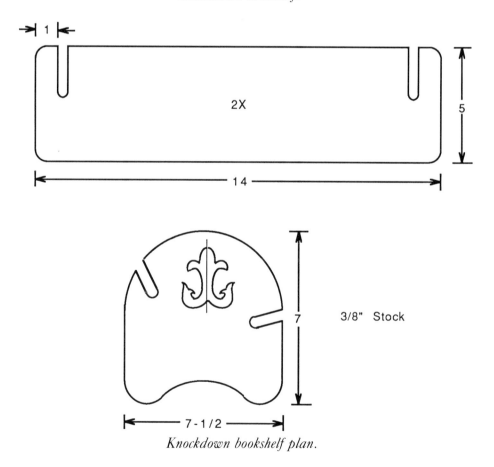

Knockdown bookshelf plan.

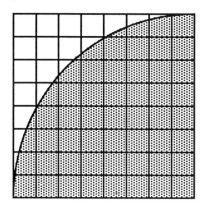

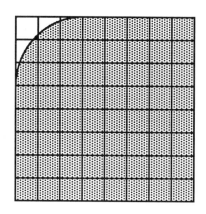

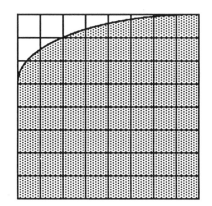

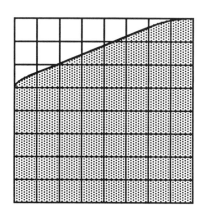

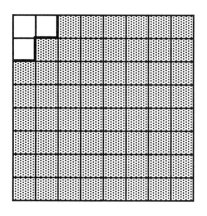

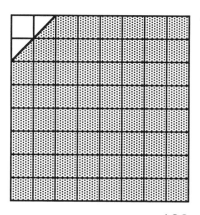

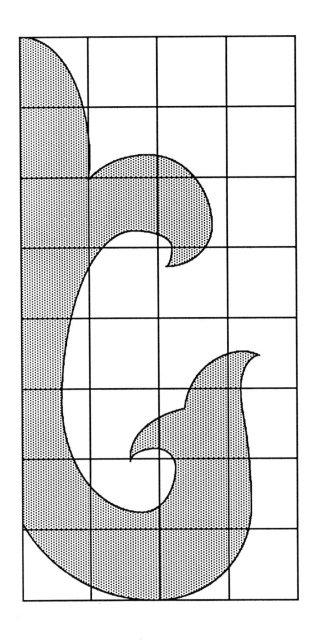

Half-pattern that can be used for the pencil holder, the adjustable bookshelf, the letter holder, or the knockdown bookshelf.

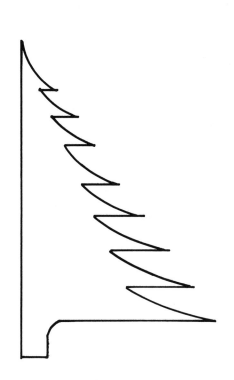

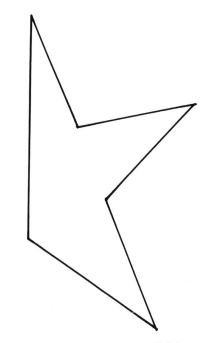

185

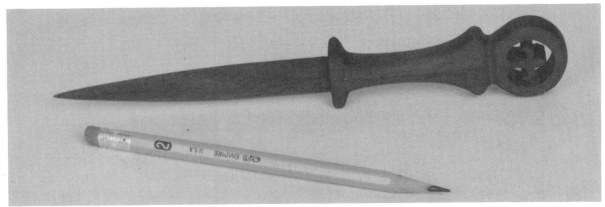

Letter opener.

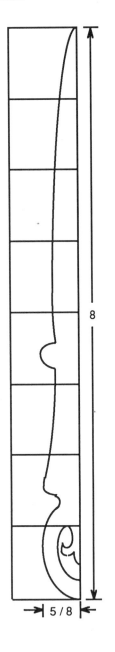

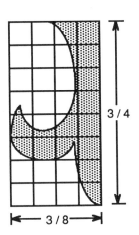

8

5 / 8

3 / 4

3 / 8

Half-pattern for letter opener.

Half- and Quarter-Circle Jigs

Many projects require either complete or partial circles. There is a plan for a circle-cutting jig in both the *Band Saw Handbook* and *Band Saw Basics*. It consists of a jig which slides in the mitre guide until the rotation point is aligned with the front of the blade. Jigs for making half and quarter circles can also be placed on top of the circle-cutting jig. An alternative to the circle-cutting jig, for supporting half- and quarter-circle jigs, is a wood auxiliary table that fits over top of the standard saw table.

The half-circle jig consists of a piece of plywood with strips of plywood nailed to either side. It is particularly useful when the design is hollow on the inside and it would be difficult to use the standard circle-cutting jig. The

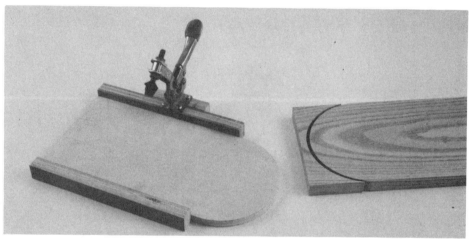

The half-circle jig has an adjustable clamp for holding the work secure while the circle is cut. The jig consists of a plywood piece with a semicircular end and strips of thicker plywood nailed to the sides.

The letter holder and the knockdown bookshelf were made by using the half-circle jig to cut the rounded pieces. This jig is particularly useful when a piece has a cutout in the middle as is the case for the knock-down bookshelf end pieces. A standard circle-cutting jig would be difficult to use for this kind of cut.

workpiece is clamped on top of the jig. The assembly is then placed on the rotation point and the jig and the workpiece are rotated past the blade.

There are options for making quarter-circle cuts. You can mark the corner of the board and rotate it freehand past the blade. Another option is to rotate

This shopmade half-circle jig rests on top of the circle-cutting jig. The cut is half completed. (Plans for making a circle-cutting jig are available in the Band Saw Handbook *and* Band Saw Basics.*)*

The half-circle jig and the completed cut.

Locate the rotation point that is equidistant from each edge. A circular object can serve as well for marking the corner.

188

the workpiece on a pin similar to the technique for a circle-cutting jig. If you have a number of cuts to make it is worth the time to make a quarter-circle jig.

The quarter-circle jig is a piece of wood with two strips of wood added to the side to support the workpiece. The jig is placed on top of the rotation pin of a circle-cutting jig and the assembly is rotated past the blade.

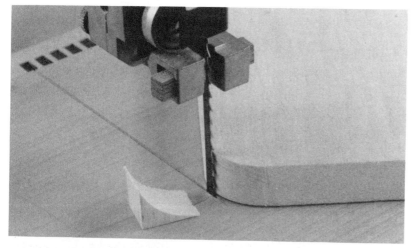

The piece is rotated into the blade making a quarter-circle cut. If you have a number of cuts to make, use a circle jig with a pin to rotate the piece.

The quarter-circle jig is a piece of wood with two strips of wood nailed to it. The jig is placed over the pin of a circle-cutting jig.

The quarter-circle jig was used to cut the corners of this knockdown bookshelf.

Metric Conversion

Inches to Millimetres and Centimetres

MM—millimetres   *CM—centimetres*

Inches	MM	CM	Inches	CM	Inches	CM
⅛	3	0.3	9	22.9	30	76.2
¼	6	0.6	10	25.4	31	78.7
⅜	10	1.0	11	27.9	32	81.3
½	13	1.3	12	30.5	33	83.8
⅝	16	1.6	13	33.0	34	86.4
¾	19	1.9	14	35.6	35	88.9
⅞	22	2.2	15	38.1	36	91.4
1	25	2.5	16	40.6	37	94.0
1¼	32	3.2	17	43.2	38	96.5
1½	38	3.8	18	45.7	39	99.1
1¾	44	4.4	19	48.3	40	101.6
2	51	5.1	20	50.8	41	104.1
2½	64	6.4	21	53.3	42	106.7
3	76	7.6	22	55.9	43	109.2
3½	89	8.9	23	58.4	44	111.8
4	102	10.2	24	61.0	45	114.3
4½	114	11.4	25	63.5	46	116.8
5	127	12.7	26	66.0	47	119.4
6	152	15.2	27	68.6	48	121.9
7	178	17.8	28	71.1	49	124.5
8	203	20.3	29	73.7	50	127.0

Index